Directing the
Children's Choir

Directing the Children's Choir

A Comprehensive Resource

Shirley W. McRae

Schirmer Books
A Division of Macmillan, Inc.
New York

Collier Macmillan Canada
Toronto

Maxwell Macmillan International
New York   Oxford   Singapore   Sydney

Schirmer Books
A Division of Macmillan, Inc.
866 Third Avenue, New York, N.Y. 10022

Collier Macmillan Canada, Inc.
1200 Eglinton Avenue East, Suite 200
Don Mills, Ontario M3C 3N1

Library of Congress Catalog Card Number: 90-38156

Printed in the United States of America

printing number
1   2   3   4   5   6   7   8   9   10

Library of Congress Cataloging-in-Publication Data

McRae, Shirley W.
    Directing the children's choir : a comprehensive resource /
Shirley W. McRae.
        p.   cm.
    Includes bibliographical references and index.
    ISBN 0-02-871785-6
    1. Choral singing—Juvenile—Instruction and study.
    2. Children's choirs.   3. Church music—Instruction and
    study—Juvenile.
    I. Title.
    MT915.M49   1991
    782.7'171'0068—dc20   90-38156
                                                 CIP
                                                 MN

CONTENTS

Preface

This is a book for children. That is not to say that children are the intended readers, although they are invited to be. Since the motivation for writing the book is to serve children, the materials contained in it are for their stimulation and satisfaction. The approach is geared toward persons of any age who are gifted with a child's spirit.

This book is the result of many years of sharing music with children, in school, in church, and in less circumscribed settings. Although my role has always been defined as "teacher" or "director," I have discovered that "teaching" and "directing" must be a shared experience to be the most enjoyable and to have any lasting value. Experiencing music (discovering things about it and developing ways to do it better) is, to me, the essence of teaching. It doesn't much matter who's in charge at the moment, since that responsibility can shift from time to time. Some of my own best teachers have been children—a role they assume naturally and without the airs we adults put on.

Given the nebulous quality of teaching, one might suppose that it is not something one need prepare for. Quite the contrary. Creating the environment for exciting and meaningful things to take place requires enormous mental preparation and a sense of structure and organization. This aspect of working with children and music is the substance of this book.

In view of my stated suspicion of the words "teacher" and "director" (and also of trendy words like "facilitator"), please forgive my dependence upon them as I proceed. Perhaps as we think about the dynamic process commonly known as teaching and learning, other less restrictive terms will come to mind.

This book is dedicated to all children, especially my own, Terry and Stephen—two of my best teachers.

SHIRLEY W. MCRAE

Acknowledgments

I can think of no endeavor of any consequence that is accomplished entirely unassisted. For this book I am indebted to a number of people who have contributed, directly or indirectly, to its completion.

My philosophy and style have been shaped by some of the leaders in the field of children's choirs, namely Ruth K. Jacobs and Helen Kemp, my early mentors—both individuals whose work and writings have made enormous impact upon so many children and their directors. I recall my very first young choir, in a small Methodist church, and my initial, tentative attempts at building an ensemble. I continue to enjoy music with children, and to learn from them, nowadays at Evergreen Presbyterian Church in Memphis. Without the contributions of real children through the years, this book would never have happened.

I am indebted to Memphis State University, my employer, for granting me a development leave in which to pursue this project full-time, and to Dean Richard R. Ranta, College of Communication and Fine Arts, for that nomination. I appreciate the contributions of the students (some of whose works appear in this book) in my children's choir course at Memphis State, and the continuing encouragement of John David Peterson, Coordinator of the Organ and Sacred Music Division in the Department of Music.

I mention my consultations with the following people: Ruth Boshkoff, Patricia M. Evans, Mary Goetze, Sue Ellen Page, and Jean Sinor. I wish to acknowledge the generosity of Michael Jothen, who graciously allowed me to use his composition in the book and to add a few instrument parts to his arrangement. And thanks are due to Scott Sutherland, who took the photographs that appear in the book.

As the work began to take shape, I relied upon the counsel of Douglas Lemmon and Sarah Jensen in revealing to me the wonders of the computer. I deeply appreciate the work of the reviewers, whose careful reading and discerning comments contributed to a greatly improved manuscript, and the support of Maribeth Payne, Editor-in-Chief at Schirmer, whose belief in the project has cheered me on.

Finally, I express my utmost gratitude to Paul T. Hicks, for his indefatigable assistance in editing, copying, and evaluating, and his unfailing good judgment. Himself an accomplished church musician and writer, he has proved to be an ideal and indispensable assistant. Our friendship appears to have survived this experience, due in large measure to his patience and good humor.

Introduction

We live in a dynamic society, with dramatic changes often occurring faster than we are able to assimilate them. We try to respond with reason and tolerance, even when we do not understand the causes or nature of these changes. All institutions and values are challenged by the diverse demands placed upon them, challenged to examine and respond.

Those institutions dedicated to religion and education, values both long venerated by the culture, are under relentless pressure to shape up to the present condition. The churches and the schools, traditionally reflections of society, are now called upon to proclaim a vision and to set it in motion. Maintaining a sense of continuity with the cherished traditions that have served us well, while shaping the future with courage and imagination, is the nature of the mission for those of us who have not fled the scene in disillusionment.

This book is meant to be a resource for the church musician, especially in Christian churches, and for college and university courses and training institutes in the field. However, this book may also serve as a reference for anyone working with children's choruses, in whatever setting. The skills needed for such endeavors are basically the same. Likewise, the book is not doctrinally slanted, though a theological and philosophical groundwork is laid. I do not intend this to be a "handbook" of quick fixes. My intent is that the reader formulate a personal philosophy and appropriate strategies to undergird and guide the choir program from beginning to end.

Some significant topics that have not been noted in sufficient depth in existing publications are considered in this book. For example, current educational techniques of school music classes are not always used to full advantage in the church choir rehearsal. Choir goals and circumstances being unique, some attention is therefore given to bridging this gap between the classroom and the rehearsal room.

While philosophy is the groundwork—the foundation—for any choir program of merit, this book contains practical and usable materials and ideas for revitalizing sluggish and uninspired programs, and for instituting new programs with the likelihood of success. In the final analysis, imaginative action grounded in solid philosophy is triumphant.

This book focuses on children from preschool through grade six. There is a special section about the Kodály method and the Orff Schulwerk, European approaches to children's music education that are gaining popularity not only in American schools but in our churches as well. Musical examples and other usable materials supplement the written text. A guide to resources completes the work.

One would be hard pressed to find a more clear-cut example of the challenge faced in our schools and churches than that of the director of the children's choir. A tradition supported by centuries of worship modes and even Biblical injunction (1 Chron. 25:5–8), the children's choir embodies our expectations both in religion and education, and the children themselves represent our investment in the future. Not even this seemingly unblemished symbol of our values is exempt from the consequences of a changing way of life. What are some of the influences that bear directly upon the continuing effectiveness of the children's choir?

1. Demographic changes, especially in urban areas, where church membership is often dispersed throughout the city, create scheduling difficulties. One cannot rely upon the routine of a single neighborhood school and community activities as the standard for the children but, rather, must plan around a variety of schedules and events. Transportation is often an attendant problem with scattered membership.
2. Mobility of families is a disruptive factor in the stability of the choir program as, indeed, in the church itself. Fluctuating membership has a negative effect upon morale and breaks down continuity.
3. The changing nature of the family itself is another influence upon the choir. The dramatic increase of single-parent and two-career families means that parental assistance is often not available at the times we need it. This situation does not necessarily indicate a lack of family support, only that other family members' schedules must also be taken into account.

In addition, some parents may not be supportive because of their own negative feelings about music. Likewise, some parents are inclined to let their children choose for themselves from the ever-increasing menu of activities available.

4. The children themselves are changing. Many youngsters are inundated with after-school activities as well as expanding enrichment of their academic life. They are not often left to their own devices. The very sophistication of their activities, coupled with the glamour of the entertainment readily available to them, spells tough competition for the simple church choir. Children expect a lot.

5. Church membership, as is widely known, is generally declining, with great losses occurring among the younger age groups. Thus the dependable source from which we have drawn our supply of children is dwindling. If the congregation, then, is the only source of singers, the prospects are bleak for many churches faced with decreasing membership and a rising median age.

6. A final factor that may be significant to the children's choir is the fluctuating condition of music programs in the schools. Where cutbacks in such areas occur, church choirs may be the only source of music education for many children. Church musicians of conscience would see this as an additional opportunity, if not responsibility, to provide music instruction to community children. And in areas where school music prospers, church choristers bring with them the positive effects of those programs.

These, then, are some of the significant factors that affect, positively or negatively, the children's choir. The dilemmas presented by some of them are considered in this book, as we call upon all our resources for solutions.

With so many conditions inhibiting success, how is it that the children's choir seems to persist—to flourish, even—in some areas? And are the reasons valid ones, defensible on theological, educational, and musical grounds?

1. The children's choir is not likely to disappear, in part at least because of the long tradition of children's ministry through music. It seems altogether proper to regard it as ministry, one that is uniquely theirs and has a long tradition to support it. Most churches have abandoned the longtime and revered practice of using boy trebles in combination with men's voices for the parish choir. However, the practice still exists in some churches, with the matchless sound held dear to church members and musicians alike. A tradition that has gone on in uninterrupted splendor for hundreds of years will not easily expire.

2. Most parents, and grandparents perhaps even more, really desire that their youngsters have a church affiliation. Whether or not the parents themselves have been associated with a congregation, when children enter the family, identity with the church takes on increased importance. For whatever reason—religious training, social opportunities, associated activities (choir, scouts)—parents feel better if their children participate regularly in a church program. For many parents, choir is a perfect combination of instruction and recreation, and the price is right.

3. The contribution that children can make to the worship service is valid and uniquely theirs. No one else can simulate it. When this responsibility is respected by the persons responsible for the program, this attitude will be reflected in the children's performance and demeanor. Worship will be authentic for the children and transmitted to the other worshipers.

4. There is a growing commitment on the part of church musicians and other leaders to train the younger members in music and worship. This trend is evidenced by the growth of professional organizations dedicated to church worship, arts, and children's ministry. There is an increasing dignity accorded children's roles, as indicated by the curricula of training institutes in these areas.

5. The church seems to be perceiving its commitment to the children with renewed insight, especially in theological education, and expanding social and educational services. Ministering to the "whole child" may be a mandate of the times to which the church, as is its mission, will respond.

This book is one such response. The observations outlined above, coupled with a concern for childrens's musical and theological development, compel the writing down of some perceptions, some ideas, even some possible solutions. Children's choirs, especially in churches, provide such a unique and available opportunity for service, learning, aesthetic awareness, pleasure, self-discipline, self-esteem, worship leadership—all very healthy objectives—that it is a worthy subject for such an undertaking.

This book will reach full fruition only as it becomes a source of encouragement, direction, and stimulation to those who share the concerns. The imagination, dedication, and musicianship of the children and their directors are the conclusive factors in building a choir that will be a source of joy to those who sing and those who listen.

Directing the
Children's Choir

CHAPTER 1

Getting Started

Promoting and Organizing the Children's Choir

"What will a child learn sooner than a song?"
—ALEXANDER POPE (1688–1744)

It is difficult to imagine a more engaging sight or sound than a group of young children singing earnestly in praise of God. Add to the tableau a beautiful ecclesiastical setting, crisp white robes, and that purity of tone that only children can achieve, and we can produce moments of high emotion and inspiration. Small wonder, then, that the church has sought to bring its young people into leadership roles in worship. The use of boy sopranos and altos, a very old tradition, is still favored in some quarters. Separate children's choirs, however, are a product of this century, and the establishment of graded choir programs is a relatively recent development.

The earliest children's choirs in Christian churches in the United States were formed to complement the Sunday school—that is, to enhance the education of the youngsters—and to provide additional musical experiences. The concern seems to have been for the children's musical and spiritual development, rather than as accoutrement to the worship service. In recent years, the movement (I think it can be properly called that) has taken on a sense of direction and professionalism, due to the efforts of the late Ruth K. Jacobs, the Choristers Guild, and other prominent church musicians interested in children's music. Simultaneously, we have seen a dramatic increase in graded choir programs, especially in large urban churches eager to enlarge their ministry to the children. Smaller churches, too, feel some obligation to support at least one children's choir, if only as a

Figure 1.1

seasonal organization to perform at festive services.[1] In some cases, the enthusiasm for choirs has caused concern among church educators and musicians, who express suspicion that the proliferation of choirs for all ages is becoming a matter of pride and that children are being exploited to increase worship attendance.

In the light of such criticism and the increased competition for children's time, it seems more necessary than ever to develop a clearly defined purpose. A sense of purpose is essential to the morale of the choir leaders, as well as a means of developing a program that is organized, efficient, and productive. One's philosophy, whether or not well articulated, is evident in every aspect of the choir program. Every director needs to work with other children's leaders in the church to reach an understanding as to what the

---

[1]A survey by the *Journal of Church Music* in 1985 reported that 28.3 percent of those churches surveyed, with memberships of 1,000 or more, have elementary choirs and that 25.6 percent have multiple choir programs for the preschool/elementary age group (*Journal of Church Music,* March 1986, 15).

choir's basic function is to be, a process that may turn out to be fairly difficult. Many individuals, and groups in particular, do not like to spend time and energy in theoretical pursuits, but are eager to get on with the seemingly more productive agenda items.

Nevertheless, time spent in such reflection and examination will pay dividends in terms of gaining the support of church staff, parents, and the children themselves. When the choir's purpose is communicated to all concerned, and especially when it has been a shared experience, there is more ownership and potential misunderstandings are averted. The director (a title that reflects this very function) is the person most responsible for the choir program and the morale of the choristers. The task should not be approached until one has given consideration to these basic matters. He or she is then in a position to guide the group in formulating goals in the most congenial and constructive manner.

FORMULATING AND INTERPRETING PHILOSOPHY

The effective teacher discovers that the surest way to communicate an idea to the students is to have, first of all, a clear conception of what is to be taught. Most of us grab on to clever methodologies, which may or may not be successful, whereas a well-defined goal may suggest a variety of approaches and also stimulate the creative thinking of the teacher.

Defining the purpose of a children's choir, or a graded choir program, will pay off in countless ways, provided this fundamental philosophy is interpreted to everyone involved and even to the congregation as a whole.

1. Those persons contributing to, or affected by, the choir program must examine their ideas about children and their religious and musical education, and determine the role of the church in fulfilling this education.

2. The temptation to capitalize on the natural charm and emotional appeal of children's singing will be minimized as the integrity of their role in worship is protected.

3. Involving appropriate people in formulating goals broadens the base of support for the program.

4. Misunderstandings about choir functions can be averted by setting goals and arranging schedules early.

5. A valuable network of communication can be established to interpret and promote the choir program.

6. Auxiliary responsibilities can be defined and delegated, so that there is no duplication of efforts and smooth administration of the program is ensured.

7. The director(s) can organize and teach more efficiently, due to a personal sense of direction as well as the security born of collective planning and support.

8. An informed administration and congregation will be more appreciative and supportive of the achievements of the choir(s).

9. Communication with the congregation and the community, which should be an ongoing process, will result in increased interest in the choir program.

What, then, are some of the considerations that need to be a part of this process? Fundamental to the formulation of a philosophy is knowledge of the various choirs' roles in worship. If singing responsibilities are frequent, this will have a negative impact upon other functions of the group, such as musicianship training and enrichment activities. It is important, too, to determine a realistic performance schedule to make sure the children can be adequately prepared. Honest examination of the motivation for using children in the service is also needed—being cute is not enough. It is unfair to force children into performing situations for which they are not musically or psychologically prepared. Each appearance should be a confidently anticipated event.

There needs to be an agreement as to the scope of the various choirs' curricula and activities. The youngest choirs will not function in quite the same way as the older ones; these purposes need to be spelled out fairly specifically. Many people view the younger choirs as preparatory groups, emphasizing religious and musicianship training. Appearances in worship services are infrequent, these duties being assumed by older children. If there is to be only one choir, care must be taken not to have an age span so large as to end up with an incompatible group.

It is helpful if worship responsibilities can be scheduled early in the singing year, probably late summer or early fall. This kind of coordination prevents last-minute problems and ensures adequate preparation time and attention to detail.

It is also useful at the planning stage to determine the purpose of the choir(s) in the context of the specific church-community situation, resisting the temptation to imitate other church programs. A choir program may be properly deemed successful only if it fulfills its unique mission in the parish. Perhaps the choir program is viewed as an expression of outreach to the community, involving neighborhood children as well as those of the congregation. Finding the most suitable rehearsal time is often a troublesome and frustrating task, and this problem, too, is best approached by considering the goals of the program in the individual church.

SETTING GOALS

Once the governing philosophy of the choir program has been defined, specific goals may be set. Basically this is the responsibility of the musical leadership, although the educational staff may have valuable suggestions, especially if the choir is regarded as a shared function of both the music and education departments.

Desirable musical goals for every child in a church choir are

1. to improve aural skills;
2. to match pitches in a specific range (varies with each age group);
3. to develop good singing habits;
4. to learn five (or more) new hymns during the year;
5. to "find" his/her singing voice;
6. to develop a repertoire of quality music from a variety of periods and styles;
7. to develop musicianship skills; and
8. to experience part-singing through descants and canons.

Some other desirable educational goals for every child are

1. to develop self-control;
2. to experience emotional release in music;
3. to know the fulfillment that comes from singing well;
4. to learn the liturgies of the church;
5. to appreciate the hymns of the faith;
6. to grow in the understanding of worship;
7. to develop poise in appearing before others; and
8. to develop a sense of responsibility and commitment.

Goals such as these give direction to the program and provide standards for those who are charged with its implementation. They should be articulated to everyone affected by the program and should be evaluated periodically. A philosophy that generates workable goals is the firm foundation upon which the choir program, however small or however comprehensive, is lovingly and faithfully built.

How, then, does a choir program actually get started? It might begin with a telephone call. Perhaps somebody at a brainstorming session suggests starting a children's choir. Well, why not? The appeal of such a choir in the worship service is undisputed and, as we have already seen, is supported by a long tradition. Furthermore, many churches, in their expanded perception of ministry, are eager to enhance their educational programs well beyond the conventional Sunday school. Such ministry may even take on an inclusive dimension, involving neighborhood children without regard to their church relationship.

DETERMINING NEED

One of the first considerations is whether there is a need for a children's choir. Other important questions that should be addressed include the following:

1. How many children are presently affiliated with the church?
2. What are the age groupings?
3. Where do most of them live—near the church or scattered throughout the city?
4. Are there children in the neighborhood, but outside the church, who could be invited to join?
5. What are their ages?
6. How can they be contacted?
7. What is the status of music education in the neighborhood schools?
8. What is the perceived purpose of a children's choir and, consequently, what are the expectations?
9. Is there likely to be parental, church leadership, and clergy support for such a venture?

Much has already been said about the importance of formulating and communicating a philosophy, the underlying purpose (or purposes) of a children's choir program. The needed support depends in large measure upon such understanding. Given the dynamics of today's accelerated lifestyles, by which children are inevitably affected, any new activity will not necessarily succeed on its own but will be dependent upon a cooperative network of parents, church staff, and other relevant church groups.

GAINING SUPPORT

The ministerial staff needs to be involved from the outset, as they are responsible for the worship services. It is unreasonable to make decisions regarding the children's participation without dialogue between clergy and those directly responsible for the choral program. Staff members assigned to education also need to be included at all levels of discussion, since the choir is generally regarded as an extension of this ministry. Any parish committees assigned to education would likewise make significant contributions to the establishment of the program. Sunday school teachers should be informed of activities and their help enlisted in publicity.

No choir program is going to be successful without the ongoing cooperation of the families of the children themselves. When the entire family is regarded as a part of the organization—by being informed regularly and invited to assist in various ways—the child is more likely to take the responsibility seriously. It is helpful, particularly in the single-parent situation, to know who in the family is responsible for the child's transportation and other needs. It is not only courteous but wholly necessary, considering the busy schedule of most families, to give plenty of notice for all events and to begin and end rehearsals at the announced times. A letter to families of prospective choristers several weeks before the first rehearsal is a customary way of inviting parental participation. A sample letter follows.

August 15, 1990

Dear Friends:

Even though we are still in the midst of summer activities, it is not too soon to think about fall events. The children's choir will begin a new season early in September, and we hope your child will be a part of the group.

We seek your help in making this a wonderful experience for all the children, since family support is essential. Many children are involved in after-school activities, and careful planning is needed to avoid conflicts. It is important that each child recognize the importance of this commitment—of time and effort—to what is a unique service to God's church.

There will be a "kickoff" event on Sunday, September 9, at 3:00 P.M., and rehearsals will begin on Wednesday, September 12, from 4:30 to 5:30 P.M. Choristers and their families are invited to the kickoff event, at which time we will review choir goals, the merit system, and all activities for the year. Of course, there will be entertainment and refreshments, too!

You will receive more information later about these activities, and we look forward to seeing you and your child there. By working together, we can make the choir a valuable experience in learning and service as we share in the joy of making music.

Sincerely yours,
Shirley McRae
Director of Children's Choirs

Further recruiting is necessary, especially if the choir is a newly formed group. Simple marketing techniques may be employed to attract attention and arouse interest. Preparations must begin in the summer, if the program is to begin in the early fall.

1. Select a theme and/or slogan for the choir season. Many churches find this a helpful way to increase congregational awareness when the theme is used in all promotional tactics. The Choristers Guild offers a wealth of ideas and ready-made materials along this line— posters, bumper stickers, postcards—to proclaim the excitement of a new choir season (see Appendix C). Richard F. Collman gives many similar suggestions for getting choirs off to a good start.[2] The theme may be incorporated into bulletin boards and other room decorations. Collman's theme "Somewhere over the Rainbow . . . Is a Choir for You" was used in a descriptive choir brochure and fabric rainbows adorning walls and hanging from outdoor poles. Phrases from Scripture or hymns often make appropriate themes.

2. Add an element of mystery. In the weeks prior to the season's first event, tantalizing posters may appear to announce that "C Day is Coming." A letter is then added each week, to proclaim eventually that "Choir Day Is Coming." All interested children and their families may be invited to this event, at which goals and activities are presented, children are auditioned, and refreshments and entertainment are offered. Pictures of previous choir activities may be displayed; slide presentations are even better.

3. Incorporate the theme or slogan in tangible ways. If it is short enough, it may be used on T-shirts, bumper stickers, buttons, pencils, and cover pages for choir notebooks. Bulletin boards and other rehearsal room decorations may keep the theme visible and alive throughout the season. If the theme is from a hymn, that hymn should be sung regularly at rehearsals and included occasionally in services in which the choir is participating. Songs may be found or written to express other themes.

4. Use many people to promote choir participation. Sunday school teachers, who see the children on a regular basis, are excellent recruiters, since there is a strong educational component to choir activities. Include adult classes, as well, as parents appreciate firsthand information. Announcements in church, including endorsement by the minister, reach additional families. The best recruiters are the children themselves, who are often willing to make an-

---

[2]Richard F. Collman, "Fall Choir Promotion: Themes and Tactics," *Choristers Guild Letters,* August 1987, 3.

Figure 1.2. CGD bumper sticker. Art by Doris Friedell.
Used by permission of the Choristers Guild.

nouncements or present short skits to advertise the program. The point is, when a cross section of people is involved in choir promotion, there will be a broader base of support. Music ministry suffers when it is perceived as specialized, elitist, and isolated from the mainstream of church life.

5. Use written communications that can be clipped and posted as home reminders. Bulletin inserts and clever announcements in church newsletters may supplement special mailings to families. Special flyers reach neighborhood children not affiliated with the church.

6. A special brochure, enhanced with illustrations or photographs, describing the children's choir program is a very attractive way to increase congregational awareness. If the cost is not prohibitive, this technique is very impressive and desirable, and more versatile than a single letter. The brochure may be designed around a theme and carry appropriate information regarding goals (stated simply and briefly), a schedule of events, any merit system used, and a tear-off to be mailed back or the names and telephone numbers of persons to call for more information.

THE KICKOFF EVENT

What, then, of this much publicized occasion? Aside from the psychological benefit of starting the year with an exciting event to arouse interest and communicate the seriousness of the program, there are other benefits.

1. The message is sent that choir is fun and stimulating, not just a matter of hastily putting together music for services. The broad educational and social scope of the program is presented for all the family to see. Such understanding will lead to increased parental support. Younger children will begin to look forward to their own choir experience.

2. The message is sent that a lot of people think choir is important. The "junior" choir is respectable and valued for its own sake and for its unique contribution. The efforts made by those responsible for the kickoff event communicate the seriousness of their commitment, which in turn inspires a similar dedication on the part of choristers and parents.

3. There are practical advantages to having everyone together at once. Presentations regarding the purpose and scope of the program can be made to singers and their families. Volunteers may be enlisted while enthusiasm is high. This is also a natural time to audition the children, as there will be activities going on to occupy those waiting to be heard. The purpose and content of the audition are described later in this chapter. (See pp. 14–18.)

CHOOSING A LEADER

Finding the best person to direct a children's choir is sometimes a problem, given the work schedule of most adults. Unless that person is already a full-time church employee, it may be difficult to find a qualified person who is also willing to take on such a project. Since the director is the one most responsible for the quality of the program and the morale of the choristers, it is important to seek certain qualifications:

Musical Qualifications

1. The director should read and write music fluently and be able to make simple arrangements and modifications to musical scores when necessary. The ability to notate quickly melodies and/or rhythms created by the children is valuable.

2. The director should have a pleasing, well-produced voice—not necessarily a solo voice but, rather, a model for the children. Excessive vibrato or heaviness of sound is contradictory to a desirable voice quality. Men should be comfortable using the head voice, although they will not do so all the time. As the children learn best from a good example, the director needs to practice good singing habits and intonation at all times.

3. Basic keyboard skills are most desirable but not necessarily required, especially if there is a good accompanist always present. However, there are many activities, especially with younger choirs, in which the leader will want to use the piano spontaneously—to accompany movement, for example. The ability to play the guitar and/ or other simple accompanying instruments is a handy skill, especially for informal activities. Recorders are also useful, as they may

be used to introduce melodies or to enhance arrangements. The children themselves may learn to play recorders and form ensembles, a possible outgrowth of the choir itself.

4. Conducting skill is essential. This means being comfortable with conducting in various meters and with accompanying instruments. The conductor's beat must be well-defined and within the range of expressive qualities and other signals that must be given. The mechanics of conducting are discussed in Chapter 7. While dramatic gesticulating is not needed or even desired, the children (and other performers) must be able to interpret the gestures and facial expressions of the director. The director, in turn, must be consistent in the signals used and insist that the children respond.

5. The conductor should be familiar with a variety of musical styles and genres. The musical menu should be varied and contain literature from many periods of history. A knowledge of these styles and a sensitivity to their interpretation are needed.

Personal Characteristics

1. The most important personal asset for a children's choir director is a genuine liking for children. This means a respect for them as people. Children, wisely, do not respond to a cloying or condescending manner—rather, they appreciate being challenged. To expect the best of children bestows a dignity upon them that other generations have not always done (as will be seen in Chapter 2). If the conductor truly likes children for what they are and requires them to be the best they can be, the response will be positive and rewarding.

2. Imagination and resourcefulness will pay off, especially in sustaining the children's interest. Childish enthusiasm tends to wane after the first excitement of a new experience, and the director who can find new and interesting ways to do routine things and fresh approaches to problem-solving is a leader in the best sense of the word. Again, working cooperatively with church staff, assistants, and parents generates more ideas than one person alone can produce.

3. Since the children's choir is a volunteer group and dependent upon support from the church as a whole, tact, diplomacy, and the ability to work with others are distinct assets. Conflicts with parents can be minimized if the leader has these qualities, which are often required in rehearsal as well. The sensitive leader will consider the feelings of every child.

4. Administrative skills benefit everyone who is affected by the choir program. Services of the church staff will require plenty of advance notice, and an organized director will respect the needs of those who coordinate and administer church events. Early scheduling and or-

dering of supplies prevents last-minute panic and mishaps. Families also appreciate a leader who is considerate of their needs by keeping them informed of activities, by beginning and ending rehearsals on time, and by coordinating the efforts of assistants to avoid duplication or unnecessary work.

5. Communication skills are so important and so broad that it is difficult even to describe them adequately. They encompass musicianship (for what is a conductor but a nonverbal communicator?) and the ability to reach the children through words, facial expressions, and gestures. Every contact is a form of communication, and the ability to talk to children, without being patronizing, is of inestimable value.

OTHER PERSONNEL

The choir director selects the music, conducts the choir, and oversees its administration. But this individual, however gifted, cannot and should not do it all. Many children's choirs have their own accompanist, an arrangement that frees the director to move around and otherwise communicate with the singers while maintaining eye contact. A good accompanist for children avoids heaviness and overpedaling, which obscure the vocal line. The piano is used for support and to add color and harmony to the singing; it should not be a crutch. The sensitive accompanist will realize when the children are faltering because of the interference of the accompaniment.

Other assistants will be helpful in administering certain details, and these may come from the ranks of the choristers' families or the church membership itself. Parties and other social events might be the responsibility of one such assistant (and committee). One assistant might be present to take attendance and help set up the room. Transportation (if the membership is scattered) might be coordinated by an assistant. Unless the church secretarial staff is able to take on clerical duties—such as typing, duplicating, mailing, and telephoning—someone needs to help with this continuous task. Finally, one or more assistants will be helpful at performance, for robing and lining up the children, distributing and collecting music, and the like. The larger choir programs obviously need more assistants, and in such cases it may be helpful to organize them into a kind of guild to coordinate efforts.

CHOIR ORGANIZATION

The number of children available for choir naturally determines, in part, how they will be grouped. If there are only fifteen or twenty children at the outset, it hardly makes sense to divide them. This situation is the most difficult, especially if the age differential is great. Children change so rapidly in these years that a difference of two or three years can create an incompatible combination. Young singers (like their elders most of the time) are inhibited in small groups, and choral possibilities are necessarily limited as well. It might be advisable to meet the younger (6–8) and older (9–11) children separately for rehearsals and combine them for performances. Music selections are difficult, too, when the maturity levels of the singers vary dramatically.

However, in the event of the need for multiple choirs, what are the factors that govern the groupings?

1. Number of children in each age group. A large group of fifth and sixth graders might form a separate choir from a comparable group of first through fourth graders. Changed or changing voices among boys is another consideration, as some conductors place these in older choirs.

2. Space. Small rehearsal rooms accommodate small choirs. Younger choirs generally require more room, as they are likely to be doing more physically active things with music. Having appropriate space available at the desired time is also a consideration.

3. Scheduling. School schedules may have an impact upon rehearsal time for various ages. After-school activities may dictate some groupings, if many of the same children are involved in several activities.

4. Purpose. The function of younger choirs is often different from that of older choirs. If the purpose of the young choir is musicianship development and religious and social education more than performance, then it needs to be separated from the older children's choir. Naturally, these goals continue throughout the choir experience, but performance expectations are often minimized in the early years.

5. Child development characteristics. In the ideal situation (enough children for any kind of groupings, for example) the overriding factor will be the maturity levels of the children. Homogeneous groups, in terms of their mental, physical, and social levels, are easiest to work with. Their interests tend to be more alike, and their responses are more easily anticipated.

The following groupings are by no means arbitrary but have been found to be reasonably compatible.

I: (preschool), ages 4,5

II: (grades 1–3), ages 6, 7, 8

III: (grades 4–6), ages 9, 10, 11

Sometimes, first graders work better with the preschool group, and some directors prefer to put sixth graders in junior high choirs. Grade levels are not necessarily the best way to determine maturity but are nonetheless convenient and readily understood by children and parents.

Very small groups tend to inhibit participation and do not provide the excitement and momentum of larger groups. Music selection, as mentioned earlier, is difficult because of limited resources, and absenteeism is sorely felt. On the other hand, very large groups are difficult to manage and encourage misbehavior. Personal attention is difficult, and activities requiring taking turns—such as playing instruments—take an inordinate amount of time. The energy level required in conducting rehearsals of large groups is great indeed.

THE AUDITION

Purpose

The term "audition" may have a negative connotation, implying possible rejection from an elite group. Such is not the case with children's church choirs, which are viewed as ministry and therefore open to all children of the appropriate age. The audition is useful, however, for several reasons:

1. It emphasizes the importance of commitment to the choir. The individual attention given to each child at the outset suggests that he or she has a personal contribution to make to the ensemble. This process also emphasizes the director's intent to help each child develop vocally and with attention to individual strengths and deficiencies. In short, the audition is a practical tool for the director, but it also establishes that a choir is a vital function of the church, dedicated to glorifying God through music. Moreover, children have musical gifts worthy of developing, and the church is interested in their artistic and spiritual development.

2. The audition provides information regarding each child's vocal condition. Intelligent voice placement depends upon knowledge of each child's vocal range and quality as well as general musicianship. This initial experience is not the only time to hear the children sing alone, but it is indispensable at this stage.

3. The audition is an opportunity to identify any vocal or musical problems. Abnormalities in quality or possible physical impairments may show up here (perhaps for the first time), as well as minor deficiencies that the interested director will want to remedy. Some of these may go unnoticed in the larger group or, if singled out, may prove embarrassing to the child.

4. Information gathered individually will result in a composite picture of the group's strengths, deficiencies, and capabilities. Thus,

planning for musical growth, music selection, and vocal development is more realistic and, in that sense, easier.

Content

Information gathered at the audition may be divided into three categories: personal, vocal, and musicianship. Personal information includes the usual data regarding the child's address, age, and school but also includes information about previous musical training, in school or privately. Measurements for fitting of vestments are noted here. Vocal data include range, quality, and independence. Musicianship skills include melodic and rhythmic memory, beat competence, intonation, accuracy in singing intervals, and maintaining tonality. A sample choir member audition form is given below.[3]

---

[3]Some of the suggestions are from Mary Goetze, of the University of Indiana at Bloomington.

CHOIR MEMBER AUDITION FORM

NAME OF CHOIR MEMBER_____

PARENT OR GUARDIAN'S NAME_____

ADDRESS_____ PHONE #_____

AGE_____ GRADE IN SCHOOL_____ BIRTHDAY_____

NAME OF SCHOOL_____

MUSICAL EXPERIENCE: Do you play any instrument?_____

Have you taken private lessons?_____

How many years?_____

Have you been in a school choir?_____

Have you been in a church choir?_____

Have you been in a school band or orchestra?_____

HEIGHT___ NECK___ CHEST___ HEAD___ ARM LENGTH_____

Figure 1.3. Choir member audition form.

For Director's Use Only

VOCAL RANGE:_____ to _____

TONE QUALITY: clear_____ resonant_____ breathy_____

nasal_____ hoarse_____light_____heavy_____

changing_____soloist_____

RHYTHMIC IMITATION: excellent_____ fair_____ poor_____

MELODIC IMITATION: excellent_____ fair_____ poor_____

BEAT COMPETENCE: good_____ fair_____ poor_____

INTONATION: excellent_____ fair_____ poor_____

VOCAL INDEPENDENCE: excellent_____ fair_____ poor_____

ACCURACY: excellent_____ fair_____poor_____

OTHER COMMENTS:

PARENT OR GUARDIAN: Please check any of the following that you

would be willing to help with during the year:

_____ Providing refreshments at rehearsals

_____ Parties

_____ Taking care of choir robes

_____ Assisting during rehearsals

_____ Assisting at services when the choir sings

_____ Transportation

_____ Clerical: typing, telephoning

Figure 1.3. (*continued*)

Techniques

Since it is important that the children be relaxed for the audition, the director should establish a friendly, informal atmosphere. Briefly explain the purpose of the audition: to determine the range in which each child sings most comfortably and how much musical experience each has had. Refrain from evaluation except occasionally, and then in a supportive but objective manner. React to mistakes without comment, or acknowledge the problem in an honest but matter-of-fact way. Sometimes a second try will be successful, but this practice should not be used to excess.

1. Have the child sing some familiar song ("Are You Sleeping?" "Mary Had a Little Lamb," "Jesus Loves Me") in a comfortable key (try several). A short introduction on the piano may be helpful, but the singing should be a cappella. Listen for pitch accuracy and the ability to stay in key. See if the child can carry the melody while you are singing it in canon ("Are You Sleeping?") or singing a harmony line beneath the melody.
2. Have the child imitate (echo) short melodic phrases sung by the director. Examples should be sung on *loo* or some other neutral syllable, progressing in difficulty.

Example 1.1

D major is often a comfortable singing key, but these patterns may be transposed as appropriate. These exercises assess melodic memory.

3. Have the child imitate short rhythmic patterns clapped by the director. The following are examples of increasing difficulty:

Example 1.2

These exercises assess rhythmic memory.

4. Have the child sing a descending major scale, beginning on c″. Repeat, going up from c′. Try the same thing, beginning on a′. Sing an ascending major scale, beginning on a. Listen for breaks and changes of quality as well as range. Determine not just the extremes of range but the most comfortable singing range.[4]

The audition process should not exceed ten minutes. All singing should be done without piano, and the director should not sing with the child. At the conclusion, thank the child and make some positive statement about his or her performance. The child will be curious about what has been writ-

---

[4]c′–b′ = middle c to the b above; c″–b″ = the octave above that.

ten, which need not be shared; however, avoid cloaking the procedure in mystery, sharing general results as desired.

FINDING A REHEARSAL TIME

The most discouraging aspect of inaugurating a children's choir program is finding a suitable rehearsal time. This problem is compounded in the large metropolitan churches, whose membership is often scattered over a large geographical area. When many schools are involved, usually there are also different schedules to be considered. The choir also competes (an unfortunate term) with a variety of other after-school activities, perhaps equally worthwhile.

Obviously, each church situation is different, and rehearsal times must be tailored to the particular circumstances of the parish. Some possibilities, if a weekday after-school time is not feasible, are

1. Sunday afternoon, late, perhaps immediately before other family activities or services.
2. Sunday morning. Not ideal, but rehearsal time may be worked around Sunday school and church.
3. In conjunction with a midweek service or dinner. Providing activities for all family members and/or a meal helps to justify a long drive.

One director reports that the major churches in her small town agreed on the same afternoon for their respective rehearsals. Thus, other groups have come to work around this day, and children are not faced with difficult choices.[5]

MORALE

Any volunteer group, such as the church choir, is dependent upon good morale for its survival. The value of music in human life, as well as its importance in worship, is discussed in Chapter 2. From an educational point of view, we can justify the church's role in developing the innate musicality in children. Such a position is rather widely accepted.

> The Creator has blessed us with many gifts, music being among the most cherished. Therefore, those entrusted with the leadership of the children's

---

[5]Carol Mixer, "Thursday Is Choir," *Choristers Guild Letters,* November 1986, 78.

choral program in the church or the related parochial school have a great responsibility to fully develop these gifts. For in the full development of these talents, the Creator, God, is worshipped and glorified.[6]

Aside from the personal satisfaction that comes from serving God in this special way and from the artistic experience itself, children benefit from extrinsic rewards. They respond to short-term goals—applause at the end of rehearsal, monthly rewards, bright stickers on notebook pages, a surprise cookie, a special privilege, a favorite activity, and of course enthusiastic praise. Festivals, in which many choirs participate, are extremely effective as a long-range goal (discussed in Chapter 8, pp. 194–96).

Some choirs work with a merit system, with a pin, a certificate, or a cross awarded at the end of the season to those who accrue the required number of points. Such a system is effective if it is simple to compute and clearly understood from the outset. Points may be awarded for attendance at rehearsal and services, deportment, workbooks, bringing new members, and even attendance at Sunday school.

Group solidarity is a key factor in morale, particularly with children. As the work of the choir progresses and their service to the church is acknowledged, they experience the satisfaction of doing things well and have fun together. Bonding occurs. This is a significant stage in the development of a loyalty that contributes to attendance and retention.

A word should be said here about the special challenge of recruiting and keeping boys in the choir. Unless they are unusually motivated because of musical interests, boys need to be convinced that choir is not a sissy activity—maybe their parents should get this message as well—and that sports and music can coexist. Boys often suffer for lack of role models: they notice that more women than men sing in the choir; perhaps Daddy doesn't sing at all. Boys especially benefit from social reinforcement and will be more interested in choir if their friends are there. If there are many children, a separate boys' choir is a possibility, although it should probably not replace the mixed choir.

Children's morale is inevitably dependent upon their sense of importance and success in the choir relationship. They respond to a director who can challenge and inspire in a caring, positive environment and make each child feel respected and appreciated. Children are no different from their elders in this regard.

USING THE COMPUTER

Many of the tasks described in this chapter may be simplified by the use of the computer. Tedious copying of musical scores and endless administra-

---

[6]Anton Armstrong, "The Children's Choir in the Church," *Choristers Guild Letters,* April 1988, 203.

tive functions may be done more easily and efficiently by this electronic marvel. Some of these tasks are listed below, organized according to types of software.

Word Processor *(anything in writing)*

1. Memos, letters, reports, publicity materials
2. Printed instructions for performances, including dates, times, meeting places, dress, music, and so forth
3. Yearly schedules of performances, including music to be sung

Data Manager

1. Directory information containing names of children, parents, assistants, telephone committee members, persons willing to drive (with phone numbers):
   Names (last and first), street address, city, state, zip code, phone number, school, age/birthday, voice part sung, parents' last name
2. Choir attendance records/reports
3. Management of music library:
   Music: title, composer, voicing, publisher, catalog number, season of church year, Bible reference, number of copies available, dates of performance, instruments
   Instrument inventory: name of instrument, number owned, cost, place and date of purchase, repair record.
4. Address labels for mailings

Keyboard Publishing *(an expansion of the word processor)*

1. Monthly newsletter, with logo, designs, special pictures
2. Birthday cards, season's greetings cards, calendars, stationery
3. Games, worksheets for use during rehearsals or for workbooks

Spreadsheets

1. Running tally of income and expenses
2. Budget reports
3. Calculations (income and expenses)

Music Software

1. Music education: software for learning to read music (award system for choir members, before and after rehearsal activity)

2. Music composition, transposition, arranging
3. Instrument control: supplement available instruments and coordinate multiple electronic instruments for performance

The computer can be a labor-saving device that frees the director for more creative tasks—which in turn can be facilitated by the use of the computer.

CHAPTER 2

How Firm a Foundation

Music and Children in the Church

"He who sings prays twice."
—St. Augustine

If a children's choir is to be perceived as a unique ministry of and for the children themselves, it may be helpful to look beyond one's immediate and specific circumstances. Let us then consider the children's choir within three related contexts: the traditional functions of music among religious people, the church's attitudes toward children, and the educational aspects of the choir. Since the choir operates within a system and a society that are dynamic by nature, such a historical perspective can lend credence to our own emerging philosophy.

HISTORICAL BASIS

Perhaps the most basic human endeavor is communication. It remains a primary force in day-to-day existence. The spoken language, while perhaps the most sophisticated means of relating to others, is not necessarily the most reliable. Artistic expression is one of the most personal, satisfying, and universal ways of interpreting emotions and ideas, and it has characterized civilizations ancient and modern. Our deepest, most intense feelings emerge as earthenware pots, or melodies, or painted canvases, or bodily movements—gestures of goodwill to those who behold or listen.

The church has historically relied upon the arts to extend its message to the world, whether educated or illiterate, across the globe or across the street. Music, in particular, has been a dominant force because of its innate appeal and because, when wedded to words, it makes an indelible impression upon the singer. One of the most natural media for musical expression, singing has been associated with religion and ritual even in the most primitive cultures. Likewise, highly developed societies, such as that of the ancient Greeks, placed enormous value on music in the nurturing of the ideal citizen.

The Old Testament gives us explicit examples of the importance of music in the life of the Hebrew people. Theirs was a poetic and imaginative spirit, as evidenced by the Biblical accounts of their worship and the literature itself. We know that the Levites, schooled in worship and music, were responsible for the grandeur of the temple rites. Levitical choirs (officially composed only of adult men but often including boys as apprentices) chanted antiphonally, with the worshipers joining in on refrains from time to time.

King David, renowned as a musician, brought ceremonial magnificence to new heights, appointing some 288 Levite musicians to form choral and instrumental ensembles. There appeared to be training for children as well:

> All these were sons of Heman the king's seer, given to him through the promises of God for his greater glory. God had given Heman fourteen sons and three daughters, and they all served under their father for the singing in the house of the Lord; they took part in the service of the house of God, with cymbals, lutes, and lyres . . .
>
> (1 CHRON. 25:5–6 REB)

David's son and successor, Solomon, carried on the tradition of splendor, and we read of the dedication of the new temple with a touch of longing. How exciting it must have been!

> All the Levitical singers, Asaph, Heman, and Jeduthun, their sons and their kinsmen, attired in fine linen, stood with cymbals, lutes, and lyres, to the east of the altar, together with a hundred and twenty priests who blew trumpets. Now the trumpeters and the singers joined in unison to sound forth praise and thanksgiving to the Lord, and the song was raised with trumpets and cymbals and musical instruments, in praise of the Lord, because
> It is good,
> for his love endures forever;
> and the house was filled with the cloud of the glory of the Lord.
>
> (2 CHRON. 5:12–13 REB)

In Deuteronomy we read that Moses chose song as the vehicle for instructing his people. Modern psychology was unknown to that great leader, but he respected the power of music to instill the essence of God's truth into the understanding of the people. He was probably a trained musician as well:

> Moses recited this song from beginning to end in the hearing of the whole assembly of Israel.
>
> (DEUT. 31:30 REB)

Then follow forty-three verses of Moses' song of instruction.

The Old Testament is rich with the songs themselves, expressing great joy and intense sorrow of the most personal sort as well as all aspects of worship: thanksgiving, dedication, confession, and petition. Furthermore, we are enjoined to sing to God in many of the Psalms:

> Shout for joy to God our defender;
>   sing praise to the God of Jacob!
> Start the music and beat the tambourines;
>   play pleasant music on the harps and the lyres.
> Blow the trumpet for the festival,
>   when the moon is new and when the moon is full.
>
> (Ps. 81:1–3 GNB)

> Sing to the Lord, all the world!
> Worship the Lord with joy;
> Come before him with happy songs!
>
> (Ps. 100:1–2 GNB)

In the New Testament there are significant references to music, notably the singing of a hymn as the final act of worship that Jesus enjoyed with his disciples (Matt. 26:30, Mark 14:26). While the identity of the hymn is unknown to us, we can assume it was a declaration of faith in God in times of suffering and conflict. Paul's well-known instructions to the church at Colossae clearly indicate a faith in the bonding power of music:

> Christ's message in all its richness must live in your hearts. Teach and instruct one another with all wisdom. Sing psalms, hymns, and sacred songs; sing to God with thanksgiving in your heart.
>
> (COL. 3:16 GNB)

In Acts we find Paul and Silas using music as a means of evangelizing their fellow prisoners. We can assume that their music was intended to impart God's concern and forgiveness for all people:

> But about midnight Paul and Silas were praying and singing hymns to God, and the prisoners were listening to them.
>
> (ACTS 16:25 RSV)

It appears that the early Christians derived their musical style from what they knew, the Jewish tradition. Being a subversive group, however, they lacked financial resources to foster choral music in a similar vein. They simply sang Psalms as congregations.[1] As the new faith developed, choral singing began to appear in both the eastern and western branches of the church. The Schola Cantorum, established in Rome by Pope Sylvester I in A.D. 314, trained men and boys in the liturgical use of music. The music itself was plainsong, sung in unison, until the art of harmony evolved much later, around the end of the twelfth century. Vocal polyphony eventually became part of the Mass and, like the part-singing that followed, required greater skill on the part of the singers. Throughout the Middle Ages and the Renaissance as well, with its highly developed liturgical style, choirs were composed of men and boys. The Cathedral of Notre Dame, in 1397–98, had an ensemble of eighteen men and eight boys.

The pure magnificence of Renaissance choral music is unexcelled. The choir tradition of England is greatly admired even today, and much of the beauty of the choral sound may be attributed to their continued use of children's voices, especially boys'. The English have placed great importance upon the systematic training of boys in this tradition for hundreds of years. The court of Edward IV (1461–83) contained a large musical staff including eight children, who were housed and fed at the palace. Theirs was a disciplined, rigorous life of study and work, but they had certain privileges and often accompanied the king on his travels. They were actually recruited into service and, after their voices changed, were assigned to a college of Oxford or Cambridge.[2]

During the Renaissance the choral range was extended to over three octaves, making possible four-part voicing, often even five, six, or eight. Nevertheless, choirs were still all-male. Alto parts were sung by men with high natural voices or falsettos, or by boys. Soprano parts were taken by boys and sometimes by castrati. The ensembles became larger, too. The choir of King's College in 1467, for example, was composed of sixteen boys and sixteen men.[3] At the funeral of King James I in 1625, the choir of the Chapel Royal, which contained nineteen men and twelve children, was augmented by the choir of Westminster Abbey with seventeen men and ten children.

While the Protestant Reformation emphasized congregational singing and John Calvin permitted only the singing of psalms, choral music continued to flourish. Martin Luther was a trained musician and encouraged choral singing, which was modeled after Roman Catholic predecessors. Lutheran choirs, too, used men and boys.

John and Charles Wesley used music to great advantage in their great revivals in England. They were known to counter violent mobs by singing

---

[1]For more information see *The New Grove Dictionary of Music and Musicians* (New York: Macmillan, 1980, Vol. 4), 343.

[2]Arthur Mees, *Choirs and Choral Music* (London: John Murray, 1901), 72.

[3]*The New Grove Dictionary of Music and Musicians*, Vol. 3, 344–45.

hymns, with the crowds eventually joining in. Charles wrote thousands of hymns for almost every possible occasion, many of which are still favorites of congregations of many branches of the Christian church. Certainly it was music that lent energy and impetus to the religious revival of eighteenth-century England.

The American church was slow to develop musically because of the preoccupation of the first settlers with survival. Worshipers came from great cathedral traditions, to some extent, but these could not be carried on in the colonies. Some religious beliefs carried with them rather austere views of music, too, so conditions were not favorable to developing splendid choral resources in the church. Congregational singing sank to such a low state in the early days of this nation that some clergymen began to seek reform and a return to "regular" singing—that is, by reading the notes. Despite a period of resistance, singing did begin to improve, and much of the credit is generally given to that uniquely American phenomenon, the singing school.

Singing schools were established to train townspeople in the art of singing, especially by note-reading. Operated by itinerant music teachers for a few weeks at a time, the singing schools were very important in shaping the course of church music. Furthermore, as musical literacy increased, aesthetic awareness of music also grew, and the movement led to the establishment of music as a part of public school curricula. Lowell Mason (1792–1872), considered the father of music education in the United States because of his monumental contributions in the field, was also active in church music reform and was a noted hymn writer of his day.

Many of the functions of the singing school have been assumed by the graded choir programs found in large urban churches. Choirs are organized around compatible grade levels, each rehearsing and performing separately or in combination on festival occasions. They are frequently used in worship when there is more than one service on Sunday. Responsibilities along this line vary widely, but most young choirs stress religious and musical education as well. While finding leadership for multiple choirs may be difficult, the advantages of grouping children who are similar in age and grade are obvious.

An organization that was founded to foster quality in children's choirs and unity and professionalism among their leaders is the Choristers Guild. Organized in 1949 under the leadership of Ruth K. Jacobs, it has grown to a membership of 8,900, with 68 active chapters in 29 states and Canada (as of August 1989).[4] Of great service to members is the monthly *Letters,* full of

---

[4]The Choristers Guild was incorporated four years later and chartered by the state of Tennessee on July 21, 1953. Headquartered at that time in the First Methodist Church of Memphis, Tennessee, the guild office was later moved to Santa Barbara, California (1956), and to Dallas, Texas (1963).

practical suggestions and materials for the children's choir. The guild has a large catalog of published music, visual aids, and other publications for the edification of directors. Individual chapters function to provide in-service training and choir festivals.

Children's choir festivals have enjoyed increasing popularity over the past several decades. Singing in a massed choir with choristers from other churches can be an inspirational and educational experience difficult to duplicate. These are often ecumenical in nature, thus adding still another dimension to the children's spiritual growth. Sometimes a guest director of considerable experience and reputation is invited to conduct and to present sessions for local leaders. Such events have enormous value as morale builders for all persons involved and provide opportunities to build awareness in the community of the importance of choral programs for children. Also, the children may be exposed to music of greater variety and complexity than they would be able to perform in their individual choirs. Meticulous organization is crucial to the success of festivals, and more attention will be devoted to this in a subsequent chapter.

The traditions of church music in America are as varied as its people. Some congregations hold instrumental music in disfavor; others employ whole orchestras as well as organs and pianos to supplement their choral resources. Some churches adhere to very traditional musical styles, while others seek more informal, contemporary, or even "popular" modes of musical expression. Almost all congregations, however, recognize the value of music in communicating their religious beliefs and in the satisfaction that comes from expressing them in song. It is furthermore consistent with the church's commitment to the religious education of its young that this appealing medium be used to advantage with them. Unfortunately, care has not always been taken that appropriate music and texts are used in their religious development. Increased knowledge of child development and changing strategies in the education of children should be reflected in the church's programs for its young charges, including those with a musical purpose. Moreover, we should remember that musical values and tastes are being formed in these early years, and children deserve exposure to the finest examples in all the arts.

THEOLOGICAL BASIS

Since children are at once the contributors to and the beneficiaries of a choir experience, it may be worthwhile to consider how they have been regarded by the church and by societies in general. Honest examination of our present attitude toward children will ensure against any subtle exploitation of them to boost worship attendance, increase church membership, or otherwise detract from the nobler goals of choir participation.

From ancient times the Jews have placed immense value upon the education of the young. They regarded their children as a part of their religious responsibility, with the family as a central force in formulating values and ideas. Early Christians acknowledged the positive childlike qualities of innocence and faithfulness, traits held up as models by Jesus himself. When asked by his disciples who was really greatest in God's kingdom, he responded by referring to a child:

> At that time the disciples came to Jesus, asking, "Who is the greatest in the Kingdom of heaven?" So Jesus called a child, had him stand in front of them, and said, "I assure you that unless you change and become like children, you will never enter the Kingdom of heaven. The greatest in the Kingdom of heaven is the one who humbles himself and becomes like this child."
>
> (MATT. 18:1–3 GNB)

"The adult-child perspective insisted upon by Jesus is still a binding claim on every minister, director, leader of music, and teacher."[5]

Religious education of the young has been a responsibility taken seriously by people of many faiths, although their methods have varied. Both Jews and early Christians seemed generally to favor loving discipline in their child-rearing, an approach that nevertheless has not been consistent throughout more recent history. The concept of original sin led to some cruel and sadistic trends in religious education, although some societies tempered their sternness with kindness and understanding. The Middle Ages saw both the "hellfire-and-brimstone" approach and a more humane attitude toward children and their salvation. Stern punishment was tempered by feelings of warmth and understanding, acknowledging that children are "susceptible to kind persuasion."[6]

Martin Luther, a scholar and musician, was sensitive to the educational function of the church and wrote hymns and catechisms for children. He held teaching in the highest esteem, second in importance only to the ordained ministry itself.[7] John Wesley's goal of Christian perfection was seen as an aim of religious education. Wesley's family exemplified the standards of educational achievement for their day, his mother having personally supervised the early education of her many children. An exception to the times, Susanna Wesley was a well educated woman.

Christians in North America have displayed amazingly disparate views of children and consequent approaches to their religious training. In the

---

[5]Edith Lovell Thomas, *Music in Christian Education* (Nashville: Abingdon Press, 1953), 26.

[6]Robert Ulich, *A History of Religious Education* (New York: New York University Press, 1968), 81.

[7]Ibid., 113.

uncompromising theology characterized by the New England Puritans, children, regardless of age, were regarded as totally depraved and thus subject to the severest discipline by their elders. Threatened with the wrath of a vengeful God and prospects of a burning inferno, they sometimes fell victim to hallucinations and emotional disturbances. The Salem witch trials have been attributed in part to the hysteria of children. Like their parents, these Puritan children endured long sermons, full of graphic accounts of eternal torment and urgent exhortations to weep for their vile sins and pray unceasingly for grace and pardon.

Later generations took on more sentimental views of the young, nowhere better exemplified than in the songs created for them. The Sunday school movement, actually born in nineteenth-century England out of a desire to teach children of the lower classes moral habits as well as reading skills, took on an evangelistic character in the United States. Songs such as "Jesus Loves Me, This I Know," composed by William Bradbury to a poem taken from a novel popular at the time, revealed a new musical style. Melodies were easy, tuneful, and sentimental; the texts, however, revealed a somber, demanding faith and a view of children as miniature adults. There was an attendant preoccupation with death and a morbid fear of judgment day.[8] Deathbed scenes were dramatized, and since child mortality was high, songs depicting the death of pious children were common:

> Asleep in Jesus! Oh, for me
> May such a blissful refuge be;
> Securely shall my ashes lie,
> Waiting a summons from on high.[9]

The idea of original sin still persisted in this century as well:

> Although I am a sinful child,
> Jesus is my saviour,
> With guilt my heart is all defiled,
> Jesus died for me.[10]

Later in the nineteenth century, militaristic imagery took over, and the little soldiers marched to moral victory singing

---

[8]For a fascinating description of the preoccupation with death that characterized this period of history, see Robert W. Lynn and Elliott Wright, "From Death to Sunbeams: Songs and Stories of the Movement," *The Big Little School* (New York: Harper and Row, 1971).

[9]William Bradbury, "Sleeping in Jesus," *The Golden Censer or Children's Hosannas to the Son of David* (New York: Bradbury, 1864).

[10]Ibid., "Jesus Died for Me."

1. Live on the field of battle! Be earnest in the fight.
   Stand forth with manly courage, and struggle for the right.
   CHORUS: Live on the field of battle,
       Live on the field of battle,
       Live on the field of battle,
           Live! Live! Live!

2. Watch on the field of battle . . .

3. Pray on the field of battle . . .

4. Die on the field of battle, 'tis noble thus to die,
   God smiles on valiant soldiers—their record is on high.[11]

The late-nineteenth-century view of children was influenced by the insights of educators and psychologists with a more natural, positive appraisal of childhood. The "little adult" with its precocious piety gave way to the "little sunbeam"—innocent, chaste, reverent, and industrious. Songs of the era, popular well into the twentieth century, reinforced this sentimental perception of childhood:

> Scatter smiles, bright smiles, as you pass on your way,
> Through this world of toil and care;
> Like the beams of the morning that gently play,
> They will leave a sunlight there.[12]

Exhortations to avoid sinful behavior were couched in precious language:

1. I washed my hands this morning, O very clean and white,
   And lent them both to Jesus, to work for him till night.
   CHORUS: Little feet be careful, where you take me to,
       Anything for Jesus only let me do.

2. I told my ears to listen quite closely all day through
   For any act of kindness such little hands can do.

3. My eyes are set to watch them about their work or play,
   To keep them out of mischief for Jesus' sake all day.[13]

Later religious education began to reflect a more enlightened view of chil-

---

[11]Ibid., "The Christian Hero."

[12]Ibid., "Scatter Smiles As You Go."

[13]"Little Feet Be Careful," *The Children's Hallelujah* (Fillmore Brothers, 1886).

Figure 2.1

dren, and their special needs required lessons planned along developmental lines with childish interests in mind. The changes in child psychology, curriculum construction, and teaching methodologies were a response to this new perception. Children's choirs appeared, along with a growing body of musical materials of artistic value, as opposed to the moralistic, evangelistic ditties of earlier days.

If there is a theological basis for the children's choir, it surely rests in part upon our perception of children themselves and our responsibility to nurture them in the faith and the expression of that faith through music. Education in the faith is an obligation shared by home and church. As we have seen, music has historically been a potent means of transmitting ideals and emotions. Words are powerful; music is powerful. In songs and hymns they combine to convey the faith of generations of godly people in an inspiring and indelible fashion.

Likewise, training in worship is a valuable function of the children's choir. While no church services today can rival the stern austerity of the interminable Puritan worship of colonial New England, we often underestimate the ability of youngsters to participate meaningfully. Offering only token recognition of their presence, such as a "children's sermon," appears patronizing and is subject to some of the same criticisms that have been leveled at those who tend to overuse the children's choir. A choir program with purpose and balance, however, can provide training in corporate worship on a continuing basis, so that the children can grow in their ability to find meaning in the service and can express their own faith through the word spoken and sung. Moreover, as opportunities are provided for them to lead in the service, they learn deportment and attitudes that in turn influence the worshiping congregation. When consistent attention is given to their preparation for worship, then the children's understanding of the liturgies makes authentic worship possible. This communicates a seriousness that elevates the choir to a position of dignity and worth and lays to rest their image as only a cute adornment to an otherwise drab ceremony. C. Michael Hawn carries this idea a step further:

> It might be said that those churches who do not have a meaningful role for children in worship probably do not include diverse ethnic groups and/or a broader range of socioeconomic situations. Our attitudes toward children in worship may be indicative of a more pervasive narrow-mindedness in other areas. Dealing with children in worship may be the first step toward dealing with the larger problem of exclusiveness in worship.[14]

Worship education, like other learning, is a gradually unfolding process best begun at an early age. For young children, active participation is essential, although the adult worshipers may present models of passiveness. Respect for the child's ability to gain general impressions while not comprehending every word rules out the necessity for condescending language and techniques. Music, by its very nature, is one of the most effective ways to involve all persons in the evolution and expression of their faith. Children are thus integrated into the worshiping community.

Finally, a fulfilled theology will go beyond the worship experience into active expression of the commitment of faith. Choir offers children an opportunity for service that is uniquely theirs. As they offer their time and efforts to learn the worship traditions of their church and assist in the services with faithfulness, they make genuine worship possible for everyone. While choir experiences should provide pleasure and satisfaction, one should never trivialize the value of the commitment involved. If the choir takes on added service activities, such as singing for nursing homes, then that aspect of the choir program and the children's support of the church are further enhanced.

EDUCATIONAL BASIS

Not the least of the areas of learning in a choir is the development of musical taste, skill, and understanding. These should not be left to chance, espe-

---

[14]C. Michael Hawn, "Guiding Children in Worship," *Choristers Guild Letters,* February 1986, 121.

cially since music education in the schools varies greatly in quality and may even be nonexistent in some communities. The fact that "choir" is a volunteer group that meets infrequently and may have fairly regular performance responsibilities makes such intentional and sequential musical instruction all the more essential. The choir as a musical training ground has a long tradition.

We have already noted Biblical indications that children were participants in the musical liturgies of the Hebrews. Likewise, the inimitable beauty of their singing has been cultivated for centuries, most often in the context of choir schools attached to cathedrals and churches. The most celebrated school was the Schola Cantorum of Pope Gregory I, established in 590 to train boys and seminary students in the musical liturgies of the church. From these ranks came Guido d'Arezzo, credited with the invention in the eleventh century of a system to facilitate the learning of chants. The Schola Cantorum eventually became the Sistine Chapel Choir, famed for its purity of tone and vocal agility.[15]

In Germany the music school of the Church of St. Thomas in Leipzig is most notable, being the employer of Johann Sebastian Bach for twenty-seven years and of Hermann Schein and Johann Kuhnau before him. The boys' choir studied a carefully constructed curriculum built around plainsong, part-songs, solmization, theory, and conducting.[16] The famed Vienna Boys Choir enjoys a five-century tradition, having been organized on July 7, 1498, to provide music for the royal chapel of Emperor Maximilian I. For their services they received board, room, and clothing as well as musical and academic instruction. Both Franz Josef Haydn and Franz Schubert were members of this remarkable group.[17]

The English choral tradition is well known for the effective use of boys' voices in their ensembles. The Salisbury Cathedral and the Lincoln Cathedral had choir schools dating from 1090 and 1258 respectively. Although some choir schools passed out of existence in the nineteenth century, Westminster Abbey and St. Paul's, among others, carry on the tradition.

Children's choirs appeared in America rather early: Trinity Church in New York in 1709, St. Michael's in Charleston, South Carolina, in 1791. The American choir school as such was descended from its English counterpart; that of St. Thomas Church in New York City, founded in 1919, is one of the most distinguished. Their curriculum was based on rudiments of music, ear training, voice instruction, service music, and secular music for public performances of various sorts.[18]

---

[15]See Linden J. Lundstrom, *The Choir School* (Minneapolis: Augsburg Publishing, 1957).

[16]Ibid., 15.

[17]Paul Henry Lang, *Music in Western Civilization* (New York: Norton, 1941), 213.

[18]Lundstrom, *The Choir School*, 33.

Most children's choirs are volunteer ensembles, often directed by volunteers and thus dependent upon motivational strategies for their success. Given the small amount of time allotted to rehearsal and sometimes an undefined or vague purpose, the director may not be inclined to take on responsibility for musical training other than of the most incidental kind. Lack of professional training as an "educator" may be a further inhibitor, although this need not always be the case.

Choir experiences may be the only opportunity for musical learning for some children and can supplement the education of the more fortunate. Certainly, basic principles of singing and music notation should be taught, along with knowledge of a wide spectrum of musical literature, including hymns. The open-mindedness of children ensures a warm reception to many kinds of music when presented positively. Educated young choristers are potential musicians and church leaders of the future at the most and enthusiastic congregational singers at the least.

Choir children also learn valuable social skills, among them poise and confidence in appearing before others in leadership or performance roles. The aggressive child must learn self-discipline or suffer the disfavor of his peers; the shy child can be helped through the support system of the group. The commitment to regular attendance and individual responsibility to the welfare of the group develops a discipline that is self-directed. Finally, the satisfying aesthetic benefits of positive musical experiences are invaluable in forming sensitive and beauty-loving human beings.

CHAPTER 3

The Children

*"Any subject can be taught effectively in some
intellectually honest form to any child at any
stage of development."*
—JEROME BRUNER

Most of us have an interest in human behavior. People and their actions tend to make the most intriguing news stories and the most appealing photographs. We enjoy just sitting on the porch or on the beach, watching other people at work or play.

Observing children at play is both amusing and enlightening; in fact, much information regarding the learning styles of children can be gathered by watching them move, sing, and play in an unstructured environment. The child at play is the child at work—there is little distinction; the playroom and the classroom are one and the same.

Educational psychologists generally agree that children can and want to learn much sooner than we ever realized. The overwhelming evidence of such research indicates that music experiences must begin in early childhood. Some interesting studies have demonstrated that even prenatal contacts with music—the musical activities of the pregnant woman—are experienced by the unborn child. Moreover, the effects of these early connections with music appear to have made marked differences in the infant's responsiveness to the environment.[1] Other evidence indicates that

---

[1]See Donald J. Shetler, "Prenatal Music Experiences," *Music Educators Journal,* March 1985, 26.

infants can imitate the "melody" of speech and laughter as early as three months. We know that "newborns can hear moderately well, can discriminate sounds, and tend to seek their source. In short, they arrive as attentive music listeners."[2] At any rate, the infant's response to early stimuli, including those of a musical nature, is an essential step toward musical perception. "Making music" at this stage includes rhythmic movement (bouncing, rocking to music or rhymes), hearing songs and nursery rhymes, and general exposure to a variety of sounds. Musical preferences and values are also being developed in this early period by positive experiences with music and other people (family, teachers, and others). It may be that musical understanding begins in a *social* context.

As far as I.Q. is concerned, it is believed that about 50 percent of its development occurs before age four; about 30 percent occurs between ages four and eight; and about 20 percent occurs between ages eight and seventeen.[3] Most of the popular and successful methodologies in current use emphasize the importance of positive early experiences in music. If one also takes into account the child's various developmental stages, the optimum conditions for successful teaching and learning are ensured.

The work of Swiss psychologist Jean Piaget has been a prominent influence in American education; and while he did not directly address the musical training of children, his ideas are keenly felt by music educators. Piaget was concerned with intellectual growth. His classification of the stages of cognitive development, which is based on the premise that children think differently from adults, is thus of interest to all parents or professional teachers concerned with their nurture. Understanding how children think and behave is the key to effective planning and efficient teaching, whereby frustration and failure are minimized.

Piaget's observations of the child from about ages seven to eleven are relevant to the elementary children's choir. This stage of development is characterized by the ability to perform intellectual operations, as new information is assimilated with previous knowledge and understanding. The child classifies information and can provide logical explanations, although governed by concrete, literal thinking processes. The acquisition of written language occurs during this period, and musical instruction usually begins as well, since it is compatible with other aspects of development in what Piaget identifies as the "concrete operational" stage.[4]

---

[2]Dorothy T. McDonald and Gene M. Simons, *Musical Growth and Development, Birth Through Six* (New York: Schirmer, 1989), 41.

[3]Benjamin Bloom, *Stability and Change in Human Characteristics* (New York: John Wiley, 1964), 72.

[4]For an excellent summary of Piaget's developmental stages and their application to music learning, see McDonald and Simons, *Musical Growth and Development,* 24–28.

Piaget, too, recognized the value of play as the way in which the young child accomplishes tasks. He believed that each time we set out to teach a child something, we keep him from inventing it himself, whereas that which he discovers for himself remains with him forever. More recently, William Hull has observed, "If we taught children to speak, they would never learn."

In the musical environment, we present the children with opportunities to "play" with the elements of music. "Children accomplish a task through the medium of play that they may not have been able to do otherwise. By bringing play into the rehearsal, we encourage children to learn in their natural manner."[5]

Jerome Bruner, noted Harvard psychologist, interprets Piaget's analysis of children's thinking into a psychological structure that he calls "patterns of growth." For him the essence of education is not so much knowledge itself but the experience of the learning process: problem-solving, discovery, symbolic thought. He describes three learning modes—enactive, iconic, and symbolic—all of which are available to adults but acquired gradually by the child.

The enactive mode is characterized by active experience, manipulation, and seeing things done—all essential to the young child's development. The iconic mode uses imageries (pictures, diagrams, visual aids, and words themselves) to reinforce and extend the fundamental learning of the enactive period ($\bigcirc\bigcirc\triangle\bigcirc$ = A A B A form). The most sophisticated mode is the symbolic, and the last to be used by children, as it is characterized by a reliance upon words to communicate ideas.[6]

The important thing to remember is that active participation is essential to the young child's learning and that it precedes symbolic experiences, which are gradually added to the environment. One does not abandon earlier modes in favor of the symbolic (it is absurd to think of learning to play tennis from a lecture or a manual, for example). Rather, as a teacher one takes into account the various modes and their appropriateness for a given task at a given stage in the learner's growth. Music, in particular, has often suffered from the futility (and sterility) of an academic approach and has consequently lost many children.

For example, expecting children to master the mechanics (language) of music before singing, playing, and creating it is antagonistic to their na-

---

[5]Michael Jothen, "The Young Child and Music, Ages Three to Seven," *Choristers Guild Letters,* August 1989, 13.

[6]For more information regarding Bruner's theories and their application to learning music, see Eunice Boardman and Barbara Andress, *The Music Book, Early Childhood* (New York: Holt, Rinehart, and Winston, 1981), or Jerome Bruner, *The Process of Education* (New York: Vintage, 1963).

ture and their very perception of music. The theories of Piaget and Bruner, which acknowledge the unique ways in which children develop and learn, are reflected in many of the current approaches to teaching music. Two of these, Kodály and Orff Schulwerk, are described in Chapter 4.

People who attempt to categorize musical behavior as a function of one hemisphere of the brain (usually the right) are frustrated by the conflicting evidence. The affective and the cognitive are both necessary for the understanding and manipulation of the tools of music and for its performance and enjoyment. For the child, then, multisensory approaches that involve the learner in creating and performing music at some level from the outset, and increasing in complexity, would be most successful.

Let us now examine the personal and musical characteristics of children at various stages of their development and draw some conclusions as to how to guide their musical growth.

THE PRESCHOOL CHILD (4–5 YEARS)

Personal Characteristics

1. Movement is a compulsion, and to expect long periods of sitting is unrealistic if not impossible. Large muscles are more developed than small; jumping and climbing utilize these muscles. Some five-year-olds can skip, skate, and bounce balls.

2. The preschooler likes to talk and can understand most of everyday adult verbal communication. There is a fondness for vocal play, dramatization, making up new verses, and acting out songs and stories.

3. Spatial concepts (up, down, inside, forward, backward) are generally understood by five-year-olds.

4. The preschooler is home-oriented, secure in these familiar surroundings, and interested in family relationships.

5. The preschool child is a conformist and likes to please, although not concerned with peer approval. The need for warmth and security is apparent, and teachers of young children often become a nurturing figure.

6. The preschooler is imaginative, inventive, and uninhibited. Psychologist Howard Gardner states that the "pre-school years are often described as a golden age of creativity, a time when every child sparkles with artistry."[7] If the creative spark is repressed or dis-

---

[7]Howard Gardner, *Art, Mind, and Brain* (New York: Basic Books, 1982), 86.

couraged at this optimum time, however, it tends to diminish rapidly, probably forever. Structured classroom activities should be balanced with opportunities for creative development.

7. Working in groups is more successful by age five, making structured activities possible. Attention span is still short, however, and the children need immediate goals and simply stated directions. A five-year-old's attention span will vary between three and seven minutes, the upper end of the time limit assuming optimal conditions. Thus a rehearsal should be planned accordingly—with a series of short, discrete activities—to maintain interest.[8]

8. The preschooler is still pretty egocentric and will demand individual attention.

Musical Characteristics[9]

1. Most preschoolers will not be able to carry a tune with accuracy, and many may not show a difference between speaking and singing voices. Singing will be light unless they are told to sing loudly, in which case they will yell. Singsong chants are natural melodic tendencies.

2. Young children do not echo (imitate phrases) well, preferring to join in at will to a song sung by the leader. "Allow young children to have multiple experiences with a musical composition prior to their actually joining in . . . Assist them in gaining a rhythmic understanding and a feeling for each composition . . . After they have internalized this, they are more likely to progress to sharing the melody accurately with their voice."[10]

3. Improvised singing tends to be higher in pitch than group singing.

4. The preschool child is fond of repetition, and the most successful songs are those which are constructed in this manner.

5. Eye-hand coordination is poor, a fact to be considered when selecting musical instruments for use by the children.

6. Movement integrated with music is natural to the young child.

7. Many preschoolers will not be able to express the steady beat to music.

8. Descending pitch intervals are easier to sing than ascending ones.

---

[8]Jothen, "The Young Child and Music," 12.

[9]For a useful summary of research relative to singing characteristics and vocal range in children aged twelve months to five-and-a-half years, see McDonald and Simons, *Musical Growth and Development, Birth Through Six,* 46.

[10]Jothen, "The Young Child and Music," 11.

9. Movement and other rhythmic activities should be geared to the child's natural tempo, which is faster than that of adults.

Conclusions About Musical Experiences

1. Include chantlike songs, focusing on the universal childhood chant *sol mi la* in middle range (D major is a good key). Choose all songs in range from d' to b'. (For more information about appropriate interval exercises, see page 55.)

2. Repeat activities often and choose songs that feature repetition of words, melody, or rhythms.

3. Provide opportunities for informal solo singing—conversational, gamelike, improvised—and for group pitch-matching as well. Turn conversations into "songs."

4. Use movement to express song texts and musical ideas (high/low, soft/loud, fast/slow). Adapt musical accompaniments to movement to the children's natural tempo.

5. Provide regular opportunities to patsch (hands patting the thighs), and walk a steady beat to music of appropriate tempi ($\quarternote$ = 120–132).

6. Provide many opportunities to experience differences in speaking and singing voices. Vocal play is fun to express many musical concepts as well—dynamics, tempo, pitch, timbre. With young children, we may need to talk about what parts of the body we use in singing. "You may have to keep reminding these young ones to open their mouths because some may forget. They *feel* they are singing. Use only gentle coaxing, inviting them to join in."[11]

7. Provide creative experiences—dramatizations of poems and songs, movements (as in singing games), additional verses to songs, and the like. Use props such as puppets, scarves, and balls.

8. Maintain a positive, nonthreatening environment, realizing that some children will be reluctant to participate at times. Avoid judgmental reactions to movement and singing.

9. Pace the activities with the child's short attention span in mind. Vary the quiet with the active.

10. Choose materials that reflect the interest of the preschool child and avoid abstractions and symbolic language.

11. Choose instruments that do not require fine motor control: hand drums, tambourine, sand blocks, rhythm sticks, for example.

---

[11]Linda Mitchell, "Discovering Music with Preschool Children," *Choristers Guild Letters,* August 1989, 15.

12. Do not ask the children to "sing out." Present a good model of clear, soft, in-tune singing.

13. Respect the child's need for individual attention. Use names freely, as well as physical contact and opportunities for solo singing.

THE PRIMARY CHILD (6–7 YEARS)

Many of the same general characteristics are present in preschool and primary children, although of course there is advancement in language, motor skills, attention span, and singing voice. Only those distinguishing features will be listed here.

Personal Characteristics

1. Between the ages of six and eight, front teeth will be missing, thus temporarily impairing diction.

2. Group work is more successful than previously. Maturity, along with the routine of school, makes possible structured activities, although pacing with first graders is still geared to a short attention span.

3. Imitation is fun, and echo work is possible—imitating rhythms and/ or melodies demonstrated by the teacher.

4. The primary child is affectionate but less dependent upon the adult leader and more secure away from home.

5. Rules and some degree of regimentation are compatible with the primary child, who finds security in routine and repetition. Individual creativity may be inhibited unless deliberately fostered in the class environment.

6. There is rapid physical growth, increased awareness of body structure, and independent movement of body parts.

Musical Characteristics

1. The singing voice is still not secure, but many primary children can sing in tune by the second grade. The range widens by about a step on each end of the vocal spectrum.

2. There is a developing sense of tonality. Asked to finish a vocal phrase, some children will maintain the key feeling.

3. Given practice, many children will gain beat competence. When this skill has been attained, they are ready to distinguish between "beat" and "pattern" (clapping word or melody rhythms).

Figure 3.1. Children with percussion instruments.

4. Motor skill advancement makes possible widespread use of the larger barred percussion instruments for accompaniment and improvisation.

5. Language development and widening interests permit diversity of song and story materials. As they imitate sounds well, primary children enjoy learning simple foreign language texts. Auditory memory increases, permitting longer, more complex echo patterns.

6. Willingness to work in a group facilitates awareness of ensemble sound and understanding of the meaning of singing in tune with others.

Conclusions About Musical Experiences

1. Songs that are constructed in a pentatonic scale (omitting the fourth and seventh scale steps) are easiest for the primary child to sing in tune. Continue emphasizing speaking and singing voices through vocal play.

2. Vocal range for group singing is now about d′–d″.

3. Continue movement and dramatization activities with music. Puppets and other props encourage spontaneous responses.

4. Use of percussion instruments, unpitched and barred, enrich the musical experience and develop fine motor and aural skills.

THE MIDDLE ELEMENTARY CHILD (8–9 YEARS)

The developing intellectual and social maturity of the child of eight or nine makes possible more interesting musical activities. Emerging independence and widening interest enlarge the field of appropriate materials and teaching strategies. The child still benefits, however, from concrete and active ways of interacting with the elements of music in an environment of creative play.

Personal Characteristics

1. There is a temporary slowdown in physical growth. Fine motor control is developing.

2. Fear of failure appears in middle elementary children, and they are easily embarrassed.

3. There is a high energy level, mental alertness, and eagerness to learn.

4. Middle elementary children need adult approval and are greatly influenced by adult role models.

5. There is a developing sense of right and wrong.

6. Sustained group work is now possible.

Musical Characteristics

1. Most children should be able to sing on pitch by ages eight or nine, and they understand the meaning of singing in tune with others.

2. Vocal range is from c′ to e″.

3. The sense of tonality is sufficiently developed to permit intelligent improvisation and beginning part-singing.

4. The voice is developing character and clarity; solo voices appear.

5. Increased musical memory facilitates longer, more complex materials and extended forms.

Conclusions About Musical Experiences

1. The child of eight or nine is ready to attend to basic vocal principles, such as head voice quality, breathing, posture, and diction. This is an optimum time for performing choral experiences.

2. Children who still have difficulty singing in tune should receive remedial attention.

3. Refinements of ensemble singing are possible with middle elementary children. There will still be limited dynamic possibilities, but all expressive qualities of music should be introduced and cultivated.

4. Harmony can be experienced vocally through rounds, ostinatos, descants, and simple two-part material.

5. Music literacy can be emphasized through reading and dictation.

6. Creative experiences with music such as dramatization and improvisation should be continued. Improvised melodies and rhythms may be notated and extended.

THE UPPER ELEMENTARY CHILD (10–11 YEARS)

The final elementary years are marked with the most appealing features of childhood while signaling some of the uneasiness of approaching adolescence. The upper elementary child has much to contribute to the musical ensemble, with vocal, motor, and intellectual capabilities being the most advanced in the group.

Personal Characteristics

1. There is great variance in maturation, especially between boys and girls (girls develop more rapidly). There are great physical changes at this age and attendant social uneasiness.

2. Language skills are well developed, and some children enter the "formal operations" stage of thought processing described by Piaget and characterized by problem-solving ability and the capacity to deal with abstract ideas and symbolic thought.

3. Peer relationships take on great importance, subjugating but not replacing the adult-child relationship. Hero worship is characteristic, but ganglike associations with peers are more significant. Boy-girl hostility is common.

4. There is an increased interest in other cultures and curiosity about the world.

5. The child of ten or eleven is given to silly jokes and is sensitive to criticism. Sarcasm is not appreciated.

Musical Characteristics

1. The child voice reaches its peak of development and, in boys, is its most brilliant just prior to change. The timbre is enhanced by more resonance throughout the range.

2. While ranges vary, b♭ to f″ is typical; a range of up to two octaves is possible.

3. Coordination is developed to permit the playing of more complex patterns or melodies on barred instruments, and some children will be accomplished performers on the piano or orchestral instruments.

4. A sense of harmony (tonality) is well developed, and part-singing is enjoyable.

5. There is likely to be reluctance to move to music.

6. Some boys will begin to experience voice change.

7. Children of ten or eleven may have the ability to evaluate their performance and should be encouraged to do so routinely and objectively.

Conclusions About Musical Experiences

1. Developing physical maturation makes possible greater breath control and more attention to the physiological aspects of singing. Children should understand the vocal mechanism and learn to use the voice properly.

2. Other aspects of choral singing (phrasing, diction, expressive qualities, intonation) may be emphasized.

3. The voice is under sufficient control to make possible very satisfying vocal experiences. The children respond to high expectations and enjoy performing, if well prepared. Soloists will emerge from this age group.

4. Continue to emphasize head voice and discuss voice change with the entire group.

5. Interest in other cultures may facilitate movement experiences through folk dances.

6. Expand experiences in reading, writing, and analyzing music, while continuing aural (ear-training) activities. Appropriate passages from music being learned can be extracted for reading, with the rest taught by rote.

Figure 3.2. Children using Kodály hand signs.

IMPLICATIONS FOR THE CHOIR

If choral directors, or teachers of children in any subject area, are to profit from the findings of developmental psychologists, then certain applications should be made from the research. Understanding the child's physical, emotional, and intellectual (including musical) development is central to a successful learning environment.

> Teachers must have a comprehensive knowledge of the subjects they teach, but they must also realize the importance of understanding the ways children think. It is not enough to recognize and label certain stages of growth, with general indications of what is possible at each level; teachers must make every effort to understand the processes of intellectual growth, and seek out ways of using it to advantage.[12]

Psychologist Howard Gardner, who has observed children reacting to a range of artistic activities, comments that the "key to children's artistry . . . lies in understanding children's overall pattern of development."[13]

---

[12]Frances Webber Aronoff, *Music and Young Children* (New York: Holt, Rinehart, and Winston, 1969), 6.

[13]Gardner, *Art, Mind and Brain,* 87.

Gardner further points out that, valuable as Piaget's descriptions are, such thought processes may not be directly applicable to the work of the artist. Based upon his observations, Gardner favors natural development of artistic competence in the early years, with more active teacher intervention during middle childhood, when the child is especially "receptive to aid, suggestion, and inspirational models."[14] Chapter 4 explores two contemporary developmental approaches that address the child's intellectual and emotional needs through music.

Purpose

General goals for the children's choir program have already been discussed. Younger choirs often emphasize musicianship training, the main responsibilities for leadership in worship being assumed by the older children. Naturally the overall purpose is common to all: growth in understanding of the faith, of worship practices, and of music itself. Nevertheless, it is helpful to specify certain goals that may vary from age to age. The following are suggestions, to be modified if necessary.

Preschool Goals

1. to find enjoyment in group experiences in music
2. to feel the difference in the speaking voice and the singing voice
3. to use music spontaneously (improvise)
4. to experience concepts of music through movement
5. to sing *sol-mi-la* accurately in the middle range
6. to learn hymns and short worship materials
7. to find emotional release through music
8. to use simple percussion instruments
9. to become beat-competent

Primary Goals

1. to learn hymns, worship materials, and songs of the church
2. to learn to use music in everyday life
3. to experience the difference in beat and rhythmic pattern

---

[14]Ibid., 213–17.

4. to express elements of rhythm and melody through movement and iconic representation

5. to echo simple rhythms (in $\frac{2}{4}$ and $\frac{6}{8}$ meters) and pentatonic melodies (*do-re-mi-sol-la*)

6. to function as a group

7. to sing in tune with the group; to match pitch with another voice

8. to play simple barred instruments

9. to improvise vocally on *sol-la-mi*

Middle Elementary Goals

1. to become familiar with all components of the worship service

2. to memorize one verse each of six hymns

3. to find satisfaction in using music in many ways, formal and informal

4. to use the singing voice well and extend the range

5. to participate as a choir in worship services

6. to experience vocal harmony through ostinatos, descants, and canons

7. to expand auditory skills through longer, more complex echo patterns

8. to relate auditory and kinesthetic experiences with elements of traditional notation to the staff

9. to develop skill on the barred and unpitched percussion through accompaniment and improvisation

10. to experience the best in church music, past and present

11. to create melodies for introits, Scripture sentences, and responses

12. to become aware of simple musical forms: A B, A B A, rondo

Upper Elementary Goals

1. to demonstrate sound vocal habits, individually and as a choir

2. to develop the solo voice

3. to experience two- and three-part singing

4. to relate literacy skills to all music being learned

5. to memorize one verse each of ten hymns

6. to improvise vocally and instrumentally, demonstrating a sense of tonality

7. to become aware of the changing voice

8. to lead in worship services with understanding

9. to extend the vocal range

10. to relate to other cultures through music and folk dance

GROUPINGS

The groupings of children ages four through eleven listed above are for purposes of noting developmental characteristics and their implications for musical experiences. Choral divisions, as mentioned in a previous chapter, are often made arbitrarily because of the numbers and ages of children available for this ministry.

It would be presumptuous to recommend a grouping that could be universally applied. Aside from the natural groupings that materialize on the basis of numbers, one should consider the overall social and academic development of the children. Language fluency, especially the ability to read, is an important factor. If there are many active young children, several small groups (around twelve to fifteen each) are easier to manage. Older children require less space and physical activity and have longer attention spans. Sometimes sixth graders are included in junior high school choirs, especially if the voice is changing. Some directors prefer to keep first graders (six-year-olds) with the younger choir since reading skills are undeveloped, especially at the beginning of the year. Most people find that children eight through eleven years of age form a compatible ensemble, at least for performance purposes.

MUSIC SELECTIONS

Certainly the selection of musical materials must be made with the maturity of the singers in mind. Some suggested criteria for both texts and music follow.

Texts

The most obvious textual element is the vocabulary, which should be within the general comprehension of the children involved. While not every word in a hymn or song needs to be familiar to the child, the overall meaning should be understandable. One's reading vocabulary always exceeds the spoken vocabulary, and it is thus not necessary to reject a fine text on the basis of an unfamiliar word or two.

What is important to remember, however, is that symbolic thought does not develop until around age eleven and that, particularly for the young child, the most appropriate texts are couched in concrete language. Likewise, the subject matter should be of value and interest and should relate as much as possible to the real life of the child. Texts that strengthen the child's ties to home and church and that encourage healthy relationships with others are valuable. Appreciation of the natural world as a loving creation of God and a responsibility to respect and preserve this environment may be fostered through texts. Christian children enjoy singing about Jesus as a boy and his relationship with children.

Finally, the texts should represent the best in poetic standards: freshness, originality, and directness. Some imagery is comprehensible to older children, but obscure symbolism should be avoided. The songs should be grown into, not out of.

Music

The musical characteristics listed above should offer guidance for appropriate singable melodies. To summarize, melodies should fit generally into the comfortable singing range of the children. These melodies should, for the younger children at least, be constructed with easy intervals and repeated phrases. The most successful songs have strong, vital rhythms with natural accents on words and the simplest syncopations. Phrases should be singable on one breath, and words and melody need to be compatible in mood. Folk melodies are often appropriate and loved by the children. As in the case of the texts, the music should be of high quality—free of trite musical ideas and with harmonic and melodic freshness. Music that the children will want to come back to again and again is worth learning.

SUMMARY

The heart of the musical experience for children lies in the active process of dealing with its elements in an atmosphere of creative play. They understand because they have acted out musical ideas and manipulated the tools of the art. The artistic experience is valid at every stage when the materials and the strategies relate to the developmental level and respect the corresponding mode of processing information. Direct involvement with music precedes but also coexists with the symbolic; the affective and the cognitive contribute mutually to musical growth. The choral experience, by enhancing the spiritual and intellectual growth of the children, becomes a unique and indispensable ministry of the church.

CHAPTER 4

Two Contemporary Approaches

"It is easier to remain Mr. Smith than to become a Beethoven."

—R. MURRAY SCHAFER

The ready availability of glamorous, exciting entertainment, especially of the electronic variety, for today's children is a fact of life. It is cleverly conceived and lavishly produced to capture the attention of young minds, although older ones are by no means immune. No matter that the nature and quality of the entertainment menu vary greatly; whether it is a well-told story in a library or a $60 million movie, a passive approach to leisure time seems too enticing to resist.

Television shows, sound recordings, and videos purported to be educational in nature tend to appropriate some of the "show biz" techniques found to have such widespread appeal. Consequently, those persons engaged in the education of children may feel obligated to adopt a similar approach. The simple church choir may seem to lack the pizzazz to compete for childish attention.

Concurrent with this influence is our developing understanding of how children learn, discussed in the previous chapter. Of special significance is children's perception of music, which may conflict with the teaching methods we try to impose upon them. In the light of the sophisticated world in which our children live, even if vicariously, it is interesting that the most successful approaches to musical education in recent years have been essentially simple and unpretentious. Two of those, of European origin, will be reviewed in this chapter: the Kodály method, named for the Hungarian composer and ethnomusiocologist Zoltán Kodály (1882–1967); and Orff Schulwerk, named for the German composer Carl Orff (1895–1982).

THE KODÁLY METHOD

Beginnings

Zoltán Kodály, son of an amateur musician, began composing as a teenager and later studied at the prestigious Franz Liszt Academy. A well-educated man with an advanced degree in linguistics, he became concerned that the indigenous folk music of his country was generally overlooked by musicians in favor of the Viennese art style and that German had replaced Hungarian as the language of the upper classes. This observation led him, along with fellow composer Béla Bartók, to embark on a mission to find, record, and catalog Hungarian folk music—amounting to some 50,000 songs in number—a work continued by the Institute for Folk Music Research of the Hungarian Academy of Sciences.

Kodály's training in linguistics as well as music enabled him to appreciate and preserve the distinctive character of the folk music as exemplified in the union of words and melody, and he also employed the folk idiom (pentatonic scales, modes, characteristic rhythmic patterns) in his own compositions. The compositional styles of Kodály and Bartók reflect their lifelong research and respect for the musical language and spirit of the unschooled population. Kodály realized, too, that the beauty and richness of the Hungarian musical culture should be brought to the nation's children, and much of his creative energy was spent in composing and arranging for them. Just how serious was his commitment to this cause is evident in his statement that "No one is too great to write for the little ones; indeed, one must do his best to be great enough for them." Throughout his life he continued to visit schools, and children sang at his funeral.

It was not enough, however, simply to expose Hungarian children to their rightful musical heritage. Kodály viewed this body of material as a language of sorts, in which every citizen should be fluent.

> Kodály maintained that folk-song is the child's musical mother tongue and must be acquired when the child is still very young, in the same manner as he learns to speak. For Hungarian children it is naturally Hungarian folk-song and consequently the music instruction here is based upon it.[1]

---

[1]Erzsébet Szönyi, *Kodály's Principles in Practice* (New York: Boosey and Hawkes, 1973, 1979), 28.

The analogy of music to language is not unique to any methodology; the Suzuki instrumental method is also rooted in a "mother tongue" philosophy. The point is that the impetus for the systematic pedagogy known as the Kodály method evolved from this perception and hinges on its implications. Early childhood instruction in the fundamentals of music as extracted from the child's own musical culture is central to the pedagogy. Not only do the folk songs reflect music of integrity and value and are thus worthy of study, they also form for the child a sense of history and identity with the culture. The fact that the Hungarian folk culture is homogeneous and relatively free from outside influences made the organization, sequencing, and implementation of a national pedagogy feasible. Kodály himself did not invent this method; it was his ideas and philosophy that made possible its development through the schools.

Today there are more than 150 Primary Singing Schools in Hungary, music being taught by music specialists. In the normal elementary schools, classroom teachers responsible for music instruction have been trained in music as well as their primary subject area and are expected to read, sing, and play. A third-grade child who could not read music would be considered illiterate; Kodály's goal of a musically literate population by the year 2000 seems on its way to reality. The Hungarian government is more interested in nonmusical results, however, and it has been found that higher standards of music in school apparently lead to higher general academic achievement. The first implementation of the method outside Hungary was in Estonia, and by 1958 it had appeared in France, Czechoslovakia, and Germany. Today it is found in classes worldwide.

Appeal

The Kodály method has great appeal to music teachers who function in a logical, sequential way and appreciate such a systematic approach. Its success with children is due in part to these hierarchies of skills and understandings, as they are grounded in a recognition of child development. Musical materials are likewise chosen and analyzed for their appropriateness at given stages of growth. This faithfulness to the abilities of the learner is in contrast to much teaching, which in practice seems to ignore the findings of educational theorists. Sensitivity to the developmental level of the child and the ability to structure a learning environment that proceeds from this level in logical steps is the essence of any good instruction. Every person engaged in teaching in the traditional sense must learn to do this. The Kodály method is rooted in such sequencing, and the components of the pedagogy are presented accordingly.

Melody

The universality of the natural childhood chant

Example 4.1

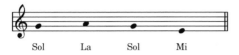

has been acknowledged by many music educators and is generally regarded as the starting point for the study of melody. Hungarian practice proceeds to *do* and finally *re,* arriving at the pentatonic scale so prevalent in world folk music and favored by Kodály because it is compatible with the musical development of young children.

Example 4.2

As this scale contains no half steps, melodies so constructed are easier for the child to sing in tune. A vocal approach, such as Kodály, naturally favors a hierarchy of melody that would foster pitch accuracy and confidence in the spontaneous use of the singing voice. While the above sequence is the conventional one, circumstances sometimes require a different progression. Older children, experiencing Kodály instruction for the first time, would reject the *sol-la-mi* songs as infantile. Some teachers, faced with such a situation, prefer to begin with *mi-re-do,* and in fact there is a substantial body of American folk material to justify such a choice.[2] Also, the common musical syntax of the music of a region may indicate a different sequence, drawn from the literature to be learned.[3] A survey of Kodály's own materials indicates still another sequence. His *333 Elementary Exer-*

---

[2]Lois Choksy, *The Kodály Context* (New York: Prentice-Hall, 1981), 59.

[3]From a conversation with Jean Sinow, University of Indiana at Bloomington, April 1988.

cises in Sight Singing[4] begins with *do* and *re* and proceeds to *la* and *sol* below *do,* the melodies ending variously on any one of the syllables.

Example 4.3

Do

Excerpt from *333 Elementary Exercises* © 1963, 1967, 1972 by Boosey & Co., Ltd.
Reprinted by permission of Boosey & Hawkes, Inc.

His *Fifty Nursery Songs* likewise begins with melodies built from *do* and *re* but next introduces *mi*.[5]

Example 4.4.

Excerpt from *Fifty Nursery Songs* © Copyright 1962, 1964, 1970 by Boosey & Hawkes Music Publishers Ltd.
Reprinted by permission of Boosey & Hawkes, Inc.

Whatever the melodic sequence, the actual pedagogy (reading, writing, improvising) is centered in that sequence, and musical materials may be chosen in part to contribute to that phase of understanding. Diatonic songs will be included at all levels, however, just as the child's spoken vocabularly differs from the reading vocabulary.

---

[4]English edition, ed. Percy M. Young (New York: Boosey and Hawkes, 1963).

[5]English edition, Percy M. Young (New York: Boosey and Hawkes, 1964).

Rhythm

There is a hierarchy of rhythmic elements as well in the Kodály method, and again it is based upon what is natural to the child. Integral to the development of rhythmic skill is the fundamental beat, which the child must be able to reproduce in the context of the music. Phyllis Wiekart's research into the importance of beat awareness in the child's overall development has led to a sequenced curriculum of movement training.[6] Circle games involving passing a beanbag, tossing or catching a ball on the beat, patting the thighs, or performing some locomotor movement to the beat (in the context of speech or music) are helpful and fun. Many of the singing games used in Kodály classes involve simple movements in response to the steady beat. We cannot assume such competence, even in older children, and should provide experiences to establish this skill.

From beat awareness come accented beats and the concept of meter and finally rhythmic pattern—combinations of longer and shorter sounds over the underlying beat. Rhythmic patterns are derived from speech and melody, and the visualization of these may be presented in a sequence:

Example 4.5

♩ , ♫ , 𝄽 , 𝅗𝅥   etc.[7]

Duple meter, simple and compound, is presented first, as triple meter is unnatural to the child. The four-beat phrase is common to almost all traditional children's rhyme and music and thus is used in beginning classroom experiences.

Example 4.6

Peas porridge hot,   ♩ ♫ ♩ 𝄽 |

Peas porridge cold,   ♩ ♫ ♩ 𝄽 |

---

[6]For information regarding training and resources contact High Scope Press, Dept. 11, 600 N. River St., Ypsilanti, MI 48198.

[7]For the full sequence, see Lois Choksy, Robert Abramson, Avon Gillespie, and David Woods, *Teaching Music in the Twentieth Century* (New York: Prentice-Hall, 1986), 82.

Peas porridge in the pot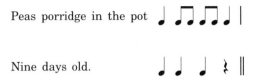

Nine days old.

Harmony

Harmony-producing activities are introduced after the children are proficient in unison singing and aural and notational skills. A sense of tonality is reinforced as they sing drone accompaniments to either *do*-centered (major) or *la*-centered (minor) melodies. The tonal center itself is satisfactory with almost any pentatonic song or song within the pentaton. Later on, chord roots may be sung to produce harmony; still later, triads; and eventually independent vocal lines.

In the examples below, the B♭ is a passing tone and does not dictate a change of harmony. The song is presented first with the tonal center (F) sung throughout, next with an independent ostinatolike harmony line (still implying a tonic harmonization), and finally with chord roots for I and V sung.

Example 4.7

(3)

I see the moon and the moon sees me, God bless the moon and _ God bless me.

Moon, moon, moon sees me, Me, me, God bless me.

The full triads (as illustrated) may likewise be sung as accompaniment when the children are able to do so.

Example 4.8

I   V

Solfège exercises in two parts may be done as well:

Example 4.9

Group 1

sol mi sol   mi sol mi   sol la sol mi

Group 2

sol mi do   do mi sol   **etc.**

Ostinatos may be combined with pleasing results:

Example 4.10

S. W. M.

(1)

Sing,   sing,   sing   to   the   Lord. ____

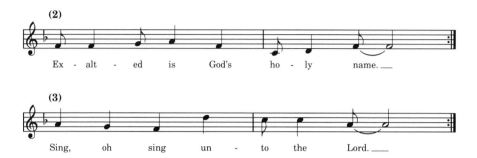

(2)

Ex - alt - ed   is   God's   ho - ly   name. __

(3)

Sing,   oh   sing   un - to   the   Lord. __

Combine ostinatos one at a time.

The following arrangement demonstrates the use of repeated four-measure phrases (ostinatos) to create satisfying harmonies and textures. With no instrumental accompaniment, the voices provide a beautiful experience with music in the most personal way.

Movement idea: There are four concentric circles, with the largest (outside) circle singing the melody, and the other circles singing the three ostinatos. Each circle sidesteps slowly in alternate directions as they sing.

Example 4.11

THERE'S A LITTLE WHEEL A-TURNIN'

African-American Spiritual
arr. S. W. M.

I.

There's a   lit-tle wheel _ a - turn-in' in my   heart, _____ There's a

II.

Lit - tle wheel a - turn - in',   turn-in' in my   heart

III.

Turn - in'   in   my   heart,

IV.

Turn - in'   Turn-in'   in - a   my   heart,

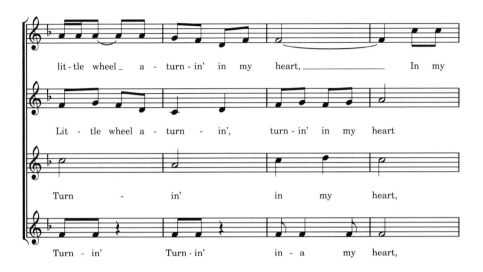

lit - tle wheel _ a - turn - in' in my heart. _____

Lit - tle wheel a - turn - in', turn - in' in my heart.

Turn - in' in my heart.

Turn - in' Turn - in' in - a my heart.

Additional verses:

    2. There's a little bell a-ringin' in my heart . . .

    3. There's a little drum a-beatin' in my heart . . .

    4. There's a little song a-singin' in my heart . . .

Canons, rounds, and partner songs are efficient and satisfying ways to create vocal harmony.

Canons

Example 4.12

I see the moon and the moon sees me, God bless the moon and _ God bless me.

Example 4.13

folk melody

Love God with your heart and your neigh-bor as __ your - self,

Love God with your mind and your neigh-bor as ___ your - self,

Love God with your strength and ___ your ___ neigh-bor as your - self.

Used by permission of Choristers Guild.

Partner Songs

Example 4.14

Carol for the Christ Child

S. W. M.

Lul - lay, thou

lit - tle ti - ny ___ child ___ By, ___ by, by, Lul -

-ly, _____ lul - lay, _____ Lul - lay, thou lit - tle ti - ny _____

child, ___ By, ___ by, by, Lul - ly, _____ lul - lay.

Text: 15th century
Music: Shirley McRae

A - way in a ___

Lul - lay, thou

Text: Unknown
Melody: William Kilpatrick

Form

Musical form is stressed from the beginning of the pedagogy, starting with awareness of like and different phrases or (a more sophisticated level of perception) similar phrases. This awareness is applied both to melody and to rhythm and, in accordance with the developmental approach, proceeds from short phrases to longer musical forms. Visual symbols may be used to identify what is perceived aurally:

Example 4.15

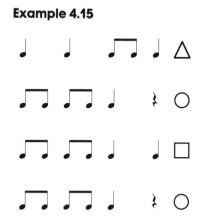

Nature

As we have already seen, the Kodály method is a vocal approach placed in a developmental framework with comprehensive musicianship as its central goal. The skills that are developed are seen as a means of making aesthetic judgments by coming into contact, in an active way, with great musical literature. Skills are valued less in themselves than as the vehicle for meaningful participation in an art that will greatly enrich the life of the child.[8] What, then, are the distinguishing characteristics of the Kodály methodology?

1. It is a vocal approach to developing the innate musicality believed to be present to some extent in every child. The human voice is regarded as the best and most natural vehicle for making music and internalizing musical knowledge. A cappella singing is the foundation for musical experiences and the most reliable, since equal temperament of instruments interferes with intonation. On the premise that the best accompaniment for the human voice is another human voice, part-singing is encouraged at an early stage.

The *sol-fa* system, derived from Italian and English systems and based on a movable *do,* is the primary means of reading pitch, although letter names are introduced after a few years. Literacy through the voice necessarily precedes instrumental study: one should be able to sing a line before playing it. The solfège approach is supported by a system of hand signs (see illustration on page 68), which provides kinesthetic and visual reinforcement, a concrete means of expressing the abstract concept of pitch.[9] This solfège system is regarded as the best way to train the ear, as it emphasizes not isolated pitches but pitch functions within a tonal system. When shifting the position of *do,* one retains the same intervallic relationships, facilitating sight-singing in any key.

2. Musical training must begin in early childhood, at least by kindergarten. Ages three to seven are viewed as crucial years in developing taste and skills that the child will never forget. Such a tenet is not exclusively that of the Kodály system, of course, nor of educators in music for that matter. But for a method that is essentially a child-centered program for teaching skills and concepts in a sequence reflective of typical growth patterns, such early training is paramount. A Kodály program can be introduced to older students, however, given certain modifications in sequencing and materials.[10]

---

[8]From a conversation with Mary Goetze, University of Indiana at Bloomington, April 1988.

[9]Based on the work of John Curwen in England in 1870.

[10]For more information, see Choksy, *The Kodály Context,* Chapter 4.

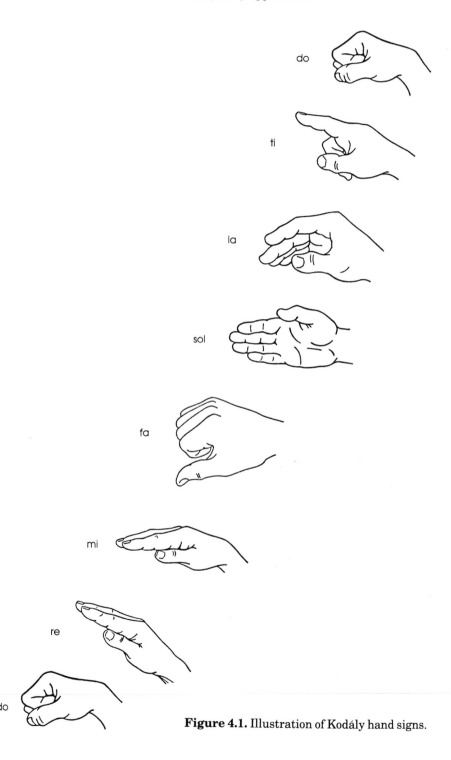

Figure 4.1. Illustration of Kodály hand signs.

3. Given the goals set forth by Kodály himself, it is no surprise that musical literacy in its fullest sense—the ability to read, write, and think in the language of music—is a fundamental objective of the method. Such ability is regarded as a basic human right and within the reach of all schoolchildren. Furthermore, musical literacy is seen as a means of interacting with music in an immediate way, to make music with others. Passive experience with music is a second-rate substitute for the active involvement that such competence affords. Impoverished is the society in which music is not a natural human activity, to be engaged in by all people in active ways.

In the Kodály method, music-reading occurs early (when the child can sing *sol-mi* correctly, he or she can perceive it in notation and take it in the form of dictation) and progresses in a well-defined order. Rhythm and melody are broken down to their most elemental levels, worked with separately, and then combined. Fluent rhythmic reading is facilitated by the use of rhythmic syllables that indicate duration, a system adapted from the work of the French musician and teacher Emile-Joseph Chevé (1804–64).[11]

Example 4.16

The syllables are useful for chanting rhythmic patterns and are used until the rhythms may be performed easily without this step (in Hungary they are used until about grade four). Rhythmic training also emphasizes movement, drawing from the eurhythmics approach of the Swiss educator and composer Emile Jaques-Dalcroze (1865–1950).

The Kodály approach, as in the case of Orff Schulwerk, emphasizes the importance of experience before symbolization, sound before sight, the concrete before the abstract. Melodic or rhythmic patterns are first presented through rote-taught songs; the chosen elements are then extracted from the material for study in notation. The child becomes familiar with the new learning by reading, writing, and creating and through reinforcement in new material. Such a sequence is entirely consistent with what we know about how children learn.

---

[11]For a complete description, see Lois Choksy, Robert Abramson, Avon Gillespie, David Woods, *Teaching Music in the Twentieth Century*, 75.

Figure 4.2. Children using Kodály hand signs.

4. The Kodály method is committed to music of the highest calibre, both folk and composed. Kodály himself was concerned with the inability of technically trained musicians to discriminate the good from the poor, and one of the principles of the approach therefore is to develop the ability to make aesthetic judgments. As has been pointed out, this is best accomplished by active knowledge of musical literature of unquestioned quality, beginning in early childhood. Singing and listening to music of great composers complements the emphasis on folk songs and singing games.

5. A key skill developed in Kodály classes is internalization of melody and rhythm. Tonal memory and aural discrimination are constant emphases as the children are called upon to use their "inner hearing" to recall pitches, identify songs through hand signs, "think" certain portions of a song while singing the rest, and in similar exercises to challenge their skills. They are also involved in the process of evaluating their own performance and verbalizing their ideas: what did you like about that, or where did the pitch sag in this song? Children are trained to become independent, functioning musicians confident in making musical judgments.

Figure 4.3. Boys using Kodály hand signs.

Use in the Church Choir

Is it possible to employ the Kodály method, founded on a highly sequenced program of music instruction, in the children's choir, where membership is likely to be transient, where other responsibilities intrude, and where time is limited? The answer lies in the director's understanding of the principles underlying the pedagogy and an ability to adapt them to the routine and goals of the rehearsal. Some specific suggestions follow.

1. Maintain the goal and effort into building literacy, even if it may seem piecemeal at times. Dissect hymns and anthems (perhaps choose some of them) for melodic and rhythmic patterns to be learned.

2. Use learned patterns to introduce new materials from notation; teach the rest by rote.

3. Include some reading exercises for their own sake.

4. Gradually expand the components that the children have learned, and continue to present familiar ones in new contexts.

5. Include some materials for pedagogical reasons, without the intention of performance.

6. Adapt, if need be, the conventional sequence of rhythmic and melodic elements (discussed above).

7. Emphasize aural skills and internalization. This is accomplished through teaching strategies that challenge the children's musical memory and independence. The director should refrain from singing with the children and from depending upon instrumental accompaniment. Include a cappella singing and emphasize listening and intonation.

Summary

The Kodály method is child-centered and dedicated to the development of comprehensive musicianship by treating music as a form of direct experience with artistic expression. The Kodály teacher works with music of high quality and uses the literature as a means of building literacy in its fullest sense, which in turn contributes to the most fulfilling enjoyment of music. Sensitive, independent musicians contribute to a more musical and, I believe, more humane society, a goal surely consistent with those of any church choir.

ORFF SCHULWERK

Beginnings

Having been asked many times "What is Orff?", I am still without a ready, concise answer. We hear the word in many contexts, usually as an adjective: Orff music, Orff techniques, Orff instruments. To the casual observer, it is just another method of carrying on a music class, a bit noisy and unstructured by some standards. The depth and scope of the musical learning taking place may also go unrecognized amid the atmosphere of fun and spontaneity.

The Orff Schulwerk is the term taken to mean the approach itself together with its accumulated repertoire. It has evolved (is still evolving) from experiments in 1948 by Carl Orff and Gunild Keetman to present their musical ideas through a series of Bavarian radio broadcasts directed at children. These ideas actually began in the 1920s at the Güntherschule in Munich, where Orff and dancer Dorothee Günther brought together dancers and musicians to integrate their arts. Inspired by folk traditions, the students created their own musical accompaniments on drums, tambourines, and other simple percussion instruments. There developed an elemental style of composition, evident in Orff's own concert works as well, based on improvisations by these dancer-musicians.

This artistic alliance was not adaptable of course to the radio broadcasts, and an experiment begun with adults had to be reconsidered with children in mind. Orff was firm in his commitment to begin with speech and singing, specifically using the traditional rhymes of childhood, and to emphasize rhythmic training. By now an instrumentarium of wooden and metal barred percussion instruments based on African and Indonesian prototypes had been developed according to Orff's specifications. Schoolchildren hearing the broadcasts presented by other children were intrigued by the sounds and naturally wanted to play the instruments themselves. The demand for participation set in motion a way of experiencing music with children that has been adapted to cultures worldwide.

Appeal

The universality of such an approach lies in its fundamental compatibility with the nature of children. Grounded as it is in rhythm and movement, the Schulwerk entices the child to explore the elements of music in the most natural (active) fashion. Its integrity in this respect has been validated by psychologists, to whom the Schulwerk may even be unknown.

> On some analyses, music itself is best thought of as an extended gesture—a kind of movement or direction that is carried out, at least implicitly, with the body . . . Young children certainly relate music and body movement naturally, finding it virtually impossible to sing without engaging in some accompanying physical activity; most accounts of the evolution of music tie it closely to primordial dance; many of the most effective methods of teaching music attempt to integrate voice, hand, and body.[12]

Furthermore, learning occurs in a framework of creative play, a pedagogical notion that has been reluctantly accepted. Some teachers do not acknowledge the extraordinary power of play and are uncomfortable in an informal setting where teacher-pupil roles are less clearly defined. The innate pleasure of music is enhanced, however, if its concepts are structured into activities that bring joy and spontaneity to the experience. The natural inventiveness of children becomes the means of exploration, and happy (and wise) is the teacher who rejoices in this.

The Schulwerk is successful, too, because of its simplicity. Elaborate equipment is not necessary, as the body and the voice are the primal means of musical expression. The rather lavish instrumentarium is really com-

---

[12]Howard Gardner, *Frames of Mind: The Theory of Multiple Intelligences* (New York: Basic Books, 1983), 123.

posed of instruments of the most elemental sort, so that even young children can improvise and play accompaniments with relative ease and confidence. The simple speech and song materials used are from the heritage of children themselves or from the folk traditions of the world. The children recognize the integrity of such literature and respond with creations of their own.

Finally, the multisensory character of the Schulwerk ensures the involvement of all children in their most comfortable learning modes. Kinesthetic, auditory, and visual stimuli are presented in activities that overlap from one mode to another. Such integration is consistent with a respect for various learning styles and with indications of research that suggest relationships between musical competence and other brain functions.[13] It also reflects the child's perception of music itself, as the entire organism is involved in musical expression.

The Orff Schulwerk inspires a kind of zeal and unusual commitment among its proponents. Whether or not one stops to analyze, as we have done, the basis of its appeal and success, the fact remains that it does seem to work. Like any other pedagogy, of course, the insight and skill of the individual teacher are the decisive factors. There are certain characteristic principles and techniques that need to be studied and understood, lest the process be reduced to a collection of undirected gimmicks. The American Orff-Schulwerk Association approves a number of college and university course sequences, as well as offering additional training at annual conventions and local chapter meetings. Orff teachers are noted for their camaraderie and eagerness for continued professional growth. Persons wishing to use the techniques and resources of the Schulwerk are strongly advised to pursue the several levels of formal training available to them, rather than to rely upon reading and or occasional short-term workshops.[14]

Instruments

The most enchanting aspect of the Orff Schulwerk is probably the instrumental ensemble, referred to as the instrumentarium. While the full gamut of nonpitched percussion instruments common to conventional orchestras and bands is utilized by Orff ensembles, the uniqueness of the sound is provided by the barred percussion. Developed specifically for the Orff pedagogy, the three families of barred instruments offer a magical combination of timbres and a range of over four octaves:

> xylophones (bass, alto, and soprano): with wooden bars, producing warm, mellow sounds but can be crisp and brittle

---

[13]For information about this theory, see Gardner, *Frames of Mind*, 122–27.

[14]For information on membership and training, contact AOSA Executive Headquarters, Box 391089, Cleveland, OH 44138-1089.

metallophones (bass, alto, and soprano): with heavy metal bars, producing rich, resonant tones

glockenspiels (alto and soprano): with light metal bars, producing bell-like, brilliant sounds

The notes playable on the bass instruments are as follows:

Example 4.17

The range of alto xylophones and metallophones is one octave higher than that of the bass instruments. Soprano xylophones and metallophones and alto glockenspiels sound two octaves higher than the basses. The range of the soprano glockenspiel is three octaves higher than that of the basses. Instrumental parts for all the barred instruments are usually notated in the treble clef, to facilitate reading by the children. Bars are removable, so that only the desired notes are left on the instrument, making possible the successful participation of young or inexperienced players. The instruments are used to accompany singing and dancing, to enhance poetry and stories, for instrumental pieces, or for improvisation.

Naturally, the instruments constitute one of the most motivating aspects of the Orff Schulwerk, since children (and usually adults) find them irresistible. While great technical facility is not required, the motor control involved does necessitate some preparation and practice as well as attention to basic mallet technique.

A basic set of barred instruments may be acquired gradually, so that a large expenditure of funds at the outset is avoided. Usually support for purchases is generated when parents see their children performing, an altogether charming scene. Choices regarding instrument purchases should be determined by the number and ages of the children who will be using them, as well as by financial consideration.[15]

Nature

No discussion of the Orff Schulwerk would be complete without calling attention to those characteristic aspects of the approach which, when used in combination and with a sensitive and knowledgeable teacher, make it unique among methodologies.

---

[15]For my personal recommendations, see "Winning Combination," *The Church Musician* (Nashville, TN: Baptist Sunday School Board, August 1988).

I. Elemental Style

> Elemental music is never music alone but forms a unity with movement,
> dance, and speech. It is music that one makes oneself, in which one takes part
> not as a listener but as a participant. It is unsophisticated, employs no big
> forms, and no big architectural structures, and it uses small sequence forms,
> ostinato, and rondo. It is near the earth, natural, physical, within the range
> of everyone to learn it and to experience it, and suitable for the child.[16]
>
> —Carl Orff

Elemental style, in the musical sense, is accomplished through the use of
simple repetitive rhythmic patterns and modal or nonclassic harmonic
style. The ostinato, a short, repeated rhythmic, speech, or melodic pattern,
is often used as an accompanying device. Not only does it contribute to the
elemental character of a piece, but since it does not require the ability to
read a musical score, the children are able to accompany themselves at a
much younger age than would otherwise be feasible. Also, instrument
playing is thus accessible to a greater number of children. One of the beautiful features of the Schulwerk is the involvement of all children in the
music-making process, not just the ones who have somehow been identified as "musical" and thus deserving of training.

Elemental accompaniments, such as the bordun (a drone, built on the
interval of a fifth, the first and fifth scale degrees), are characteristic of Orff
orchestrations. The resulting archaic sound is very effective with the pentatonic and modal melodies often used. Again, by virtue of its being a repe-
titious pattern, it forms an easy accompaniment for the children. The simple bordun may be of four types. Illustrations are in the key of C.

Example 4.18

CHORD   LEVEL   BROKEN CHORD   CROSSOVER

When diatonic melodies call for changing harmonies, the third of the chord
is often omitted, preserving the elemental character:

Example 4.19

I   V   I   I   VII   I
     (F major)   (D minor)

---

[16]From a speech given by Carl Orff at the opening of the Orff Institute in Salzburg on October
25, 1963, and published by B. Schotts Söhne, Mainz, from the Orff Institute's *Jahrbuch*, 1963.
The translation is by Margaret Murray.

The following arrangements serve as examples of some of the above elemental accompaniment styles.

"Suo Gan," a *do-re-mi* song from the Welsh tradition, is presented in two orchestrations: (1) a simple bordun accompaniment of the chord type, suitable for young children, and (2) a I–V accompaniment in the elemental style. Other instruments are added for support and color.

For an explanation of instrumental symbols used in the musical examples in this chapter, please refer to Appendix D, page 222.

Orchestration for young children:

Example 4.20

SUO GAN (See-oh-gahn)

Welsh melody
arr. S. W. M.

* Play any two notes in the pentatonic scale of G (C and F removed). The effect is one of a tone cluster.

1. Suo gan, Eastern star,
   Suo gan, from afar,
   Suo gan, shepherds sing,
   Suo gan, newborn King.

2. Suo gan, from above,
   Suo gan, song of love,
   Suo gan, blessed morn,
   Suo gan, Christ is born.

Orchestration for older children:

Example 4.21

SUO GAN (see-oh-gahn)

Welsh melody
arr. by S. W. M.

The following example uses the refrain of a hymn as the basis for an extended rondo. The accompaniment is simple and childlike, allowing for a variety of texture and color in the sections created by the children:

Example 4.22

ALL THINGS BRIGHT AND BEAUTIFUL

Cecil Frances Alexander

S. W. M.

B sections: verses of the hymn, spoken expressively and without regard to rhythm. These are prepared by groups of children, who experiment with dynamics, pitch, movement, and instruments to enhance the text. The piece is performed as a rondo, with the song as A, group settings of verses in between:

A B A C A D A E A

1. Each little flower that opens, each little bird that sings,
   God made their glowing colors and made their tiny wings.

2. The purple-headed mountains, the river running by,
   The sunset and the morning that brightens up the sky.

3. The cold wind in the winter, the pleasant summer sun,
   The ripe fruits in the garden: God made them every one.

4. God gave us eyes to see them, and lips that we might tell
   How great is God Almighty, who has made all things well.

II. Developmental Approach

We have already seen how the Schulwerk accommodates the learning levels and styles of all kinds of children. It is said that the sequence of learning parallels that of the historical development of music itself; rhythm was the first element to appear, followed by melody and eventually by harmony.

Rhythm

Orff recognized the fundamental nature of rhythm and the absolute necessity to respond to it through movement. "It is difficult to teach rhythm. One can only release it. Rhythm is no abstract concept, it is life itself. Rhythm is active and produces effects, it is the unifying power of language, movement, and music."[17]

Consequently, rhythm is one of the most compelling features of music in the Orff style, and its study is emphasized at every level of instruction. The child is guided through a carefully sequenced repertoire of rhythmic patterns, first by imitation, then by improvisation, and finally by notation. A rhythmic vocabulary is developed as the children echo patterns presented by the teacher.

Example 4.23

---

[17]Carl Orff, *The Schulwerk,* tr. Margaret Murray (New York: Schott, n.d.), 17.

The patterns may be imitated vocally, on body instruments (clapping, snapping, patschen or thigh-slapping, stamping), or on percussion instruments. Using the body as a musical instrument is elemental and natural to the child, and thus a nonthreatening way to experience rhythm pattern and steady beat. It is also an effective way to develop accompaniments for speech and song, as well as a successful means of preparing for instrumental patterns. Rhythm canons may be performed spontaneously, with the children responding four beats behind the leader, or as a learned sequence:

Example 4.24

Perform in canon twice, the first time standing, the second time sitting.

Rhythms derived from speech patterns are explored, such as names of the children themselves.

Example 4.25

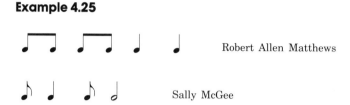

Name patterns may be used in gamelike settings and grouped in sets for rhythmic phrases. The following song may be used (with or without the accompaniment) as the A section of a giant rondo. The children are seated on the floor in a circle. Following the song, four children in turn clap and/or speak their names in rhythm. Again the song is sung, and the name game continues around the circle until all children have had a turn:

Example 4.26

* word patterns to facilitate playing correct rhythm

In the following example, the song serves as the A section. The children may create a section of names (spoken, clapped, or played on instruments) that have been placed in a pleasing order. They may use names of people they know, Biblical characters, famous people, or people such as the postal carrier, the florist, or a neighbor. These speech/percussion sections serve as contrasting elements, returning to the song again to complete the form: A B A C A.

Example 4.27

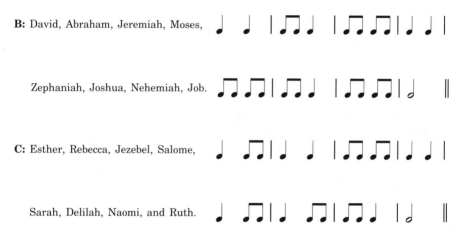

B: David, Abraham, Jeremiah, Moses,

Zephaniah, Joshua, Nehemiah, Job.

C: Esther, Rebecca, Jezebel, Salome,

Sarah, Delilah, Naomi, and Ruth.

Example 4.28

S. W. M.

Some-bod-y's knock-ing at my door, Who can it be?

Poems and rhymes of childhood are usually highly rhythmic, inviting rhythmic play and the cultivation of expressive speech. Many of the properties and expressive qualities of music are also present in speech—rhythm, pitch, texture, timbre, dynamics, tempo. Thus choral speech can be a genuine musical event in the aesthetic sense, as the children explore ways to add drama, variety, and interest to their speech. The following arrangement based on Psalm 96 provides an opportunity to use the spoken word in a liturgical setting.

Example 4.29

SPEECH INTROIT

Based on Psalm 96   S. W. M.

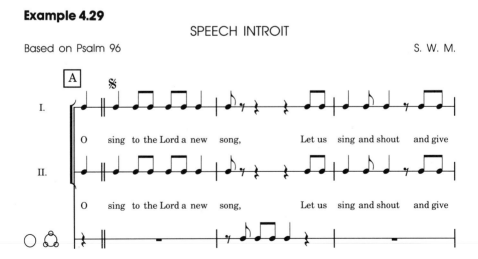

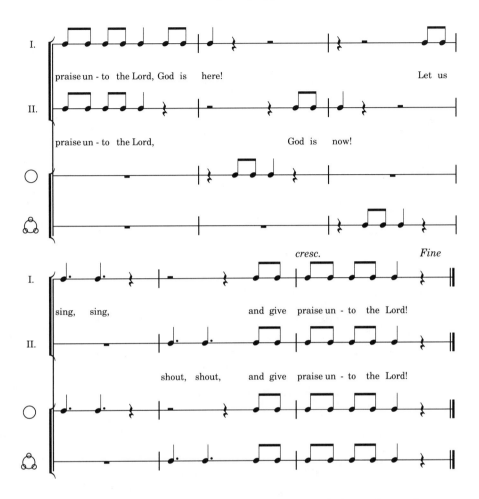

(Spoken dramatically and freely, without a feeling of meter)

This is a time for celebration!

(solo) We shall not forget the *old* songs we have loved . . .
(solo) But let us create *new* songs to praise God!

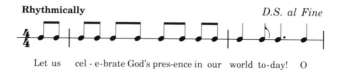

Let us   cel - e-brate God's pres-ence in our world to-day!   O

Form: A B A

Poems may also be enhanced with instrumental color and as a stimulus and for movement for vocal and motor development in the rehearsal.

Example 4.30

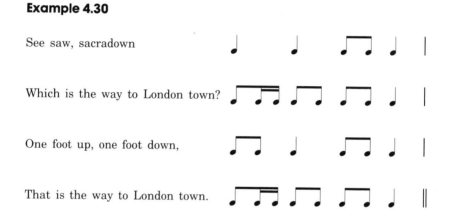

See saw, sacradown

Which is the way to London town?

One foot up, one foot down,

That is the way to London town.

The above poem may be spoken in a variety of styles: softest voices, with a crescendo or decrescendo, in different tempi, in high (pitched) voices, in low voices, in canon, or in British accent, to encourage expressive and imaginative uses of the voice in musical ways. Body instruments or percussion instruments may be added as follows:

>   see saw sacradown—syllables clapped, or played on wood block
>
>   London town—syllables patsched, or played on triangle
>
>   up—snapped, or a glissando up on a glockenspiel
>
>   down—stamped, or a glissando down on a glockenspiel

Movement may be added, as the children decide how they will go to London town (names of other towns may be substituted). The entire choir may move in the same manner, or children may choose their own styles from a list, as:

Figure 4.4. Temple blocks in use.

walk very tall	walk with giant steps	tiptoe
skip	jog	march
walk backward	walk on heels	hopscotch

Since singing may be regarded as an extension of speech, the manipulation of the speaking voice is also a useful tool for helping the child find and cultivate the singing voice without the embarrassment associated with the inability to sing in tune. In any event, the Orff Schulwerk emphasizes this kind of activity as legitimate musical expression. There will be more ideas for voice exploration in Chapter 7.

Melody

Just as rhythm is presented in an ordered sequence according to the child's developmental levels, melody is carefully introduced beginning with the natural chants common to childhood, using the tones *sol, mi,* and *la.*

Example 4.31

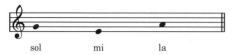

The children use these familiar pitches routinely to "converse" (improvise), later extending the tonal repertoire to include *re* and *do* (creating a pentatonic scale)

Example 4.32

and eventually *fa* and *ti* (the diatonic scale).

Example 4.33

Echo singing is a regular event, in the manner of rhythmic imitation to develop the ear as well as to introduce songs. For example, the song "Suo Gan" (see above) may be presented in a manner designed to develop the ear, with the children echoing the three melodic patterns that constitute the piece, on solfège syllables or some neutral syllable (to maintain focus on melody, not words).

Example 4.34

This aural work may be reinforced at some point with the melodies in notation, adding a visual component as well as skill development. Singing the motives separately and then in sequence (much like putting a puzzle back together) emphasizes the concept of musical form.

Harmony

As melodies are combined or provided with instrumental accompaniments, harmony is produced. Simple borduns (described above) create an elemental, droning background based on the tonic harmony and that does not change. When melodies call for chord changes, the elemental style characteristic of the Orff sound requires that the harmonies remain open and uncluttered. Certain ethnic and cultural materials, however, are exceptions to this approach to orchestration. Also, modal melodies and harmonizations add an archaic richness to the children's musical vocabularies.

A call to worship harmonized in the Dorian mode and featuring mixed meters, lending vitality to the piece:

Example 4.35

THIS IS THE DAY

S. W. M.

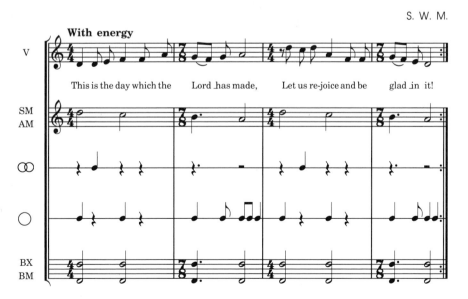

A Christmas carol in the natural minor (transposed Aeolian) and with a haunting, plaintive character. The melody, composed of three four-measure phrases, is accompanied by four-measure ostinatos:

Example 4.36

There I met an old man a - long the way, O

2. I spoke to the old man who said to me,
   "Listen to the bird singing in the tree."
   O sing we all Noel, Noel, Noel.

3. Listen to the bird singing sweet and clear,
   Singing out good tidings for all to hear.
   O sing we all Noel, Noel, Noel.

From Imitation to Improvisation

A distinctive aspect of the developmental approach of the Orff Schulwerk is the progression from imitation to improvisation. It is necessary that the children have a repertoire of musical ideas from which to draw and that they alter or extend into little creations of their own. Clapping a spontaneous rhythm pattern is a valid achievement as well as a significant step toward longer or more sophisticated improvisations. But even this primal attempt depends upon a "catalog" of musical ideas and confidence acquired through previous experiences. Creativity must be nurtured from an early age, lest the children lose their willingness to be inventive. Mostly this goal is met by an ongoing process of music-making, in which they feel free to risk their own ideas without fear of embarrassment or criticism. The teacher provides the structure, allowing for small choices, and all responses are acceptable. The children develop aesthetic judgment as they gain practice and as refinements are made.

Improvisation, or spontaneous music-making, may take the form of vocal sounds (nonsense), body percussion, unpitched percussion instruments, barred instruments, or singing. Children may begin by finishing a phrase begun by the teacher, usually eight beats in length.

Example 4.37

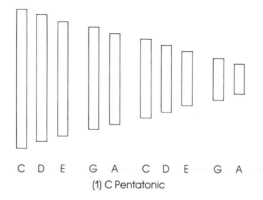

As skills and confidence increase, as well as the musical vocabulary, the length of the improvisations may be extended. When improvising on the barred instruments, a pentatonic scale (fourth and seventh steps removed) should be used to avoid dissonance. The instrument would thus be set up as in Figure 4.5, in the keys of C, F, and G respectively.

C D E   G A   C D E   G A
(1) C Pentatonic

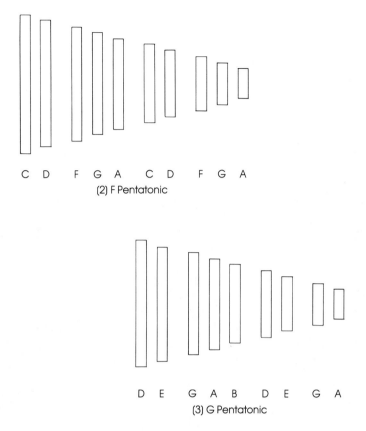

C D   F G A   C D   F G A
(2) F Pentatonic

D E   G A B   D E   G A
(3) G Pentatonic

Figure 4.5. Pentatonic arrangement of barred percussion instruments.

Children will be most secure if in early attempts they improvise in groups, moving as they are willing to individual responses.

The following song may be used as the basis for group improvisation on the barred instruments, which are set up in G pentatonic (3 above). This arrangement enables many children to play at once and to play any notes at will, without creating dissonance. The four groups of instrument players, corresponding to key words in the song, improvise in turn to their assigned rhythm. The improvisations are each eight beats in length, so that the total time (the B section) equals that of the song itself. The form thus becomes

A: song with accompaniment

B: improvisations (in order: BX/BM, SM/AM, SX/AX, SG/AG)

A: song with accompaniment

Example 4.38   LITTLE WIND

Kate Greenaway   S. W. M.

Early attempts at improvisation are more successful if some structure is provided. In this case, the melodic structure is the G pentatonic scale, and there is a rhythmic structure as well. As the children become confident in their music-making, the structures may be changed or made less constricting.

In any event, musical creations small or large by the children themselves cannot fail to inspire excitement and pride among those who create and those who observe.

Figure 4.6. Children playing various percussion instruments.

Involvement of All Children

Visitors to Orff classes often remark with amazement that every child is involved somehow in all aspects of the experience. This is truly one of the most significant factors in the success of the approach. All children, for example, are prepared (through speech or body percussion or both) to play an accompaniment for which there may be only one or two available instruments. All children learn all elements of the activity—singing, speech, movement, instruments. Moreover, the children are often required to do more than one thing at once (sing and play, sing and move)—no easy task. Likewise, the variety of tasks involved in a typical activity enables every child to be competent and fulfilled at some level.

Concrete to Abstract

Musical literacy is generally considered a requisite of the competent musician, although there are many examples to contradict this. Moreover, a reliable system of notation is relatively new, musical expression having flourished for centuries without it. Nevertheless, educators in this country have consistently equated literacy with successful programs, however their methods may have differed. Some systems of music instruction place music-reading at the top of the list of skills to be mastered; others appear to take a more casual approach.

The Orff Schulwerk is based on the premise that experience precedes symbolic learning, that the concrete leads to the abstract. This idea is not unique to the Schulwerk, of course, but it is central to the process of developing musicianship in its comprehensive sense: being comfortable with all the tools of music-making, with improvisation, and with conventional systems of notation. Therefore, as the children require the mechanics of notation, in order to recall their music, the elements are introduced, slowly but systematically and in many contexts. Careful attention is given to the development of reading skills, but they are related to real musical experiences as much as possible. In the following little canon, young children may create movements to correspond to the four basic note values presented (the whole note may be difficult). Word patterns could reinforce the concept:

Example 4.39

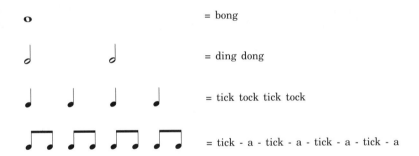

A glockenspiel may double the "cuckoo" motive each time it occurs.

Example 4.40

A simple bordun may accompany (Example 4.40). Older children can perform the song in canon as well as the accompaniment patterns.

Example 4.41

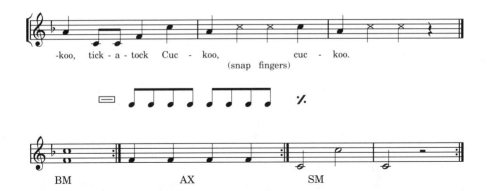

Occasional reading games may be used to reinforce rhythmic notation skills in a musical (performance) context.

Example 4.42

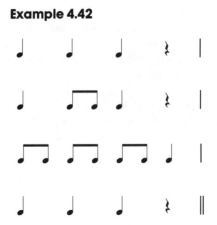

Process:

1. Place the rhythms on the board or on a large chart.
2. Clap them one line at a time; vary body instruments.
3. Perform in canon.
4. Play on percussion instruments.
5. For older children, ♩ may be played by drums, 𝄽 by metal instruments, and ♫ by wooden instruments.
6. For "inner hearing," play the entire piece, omitting (but thinking) the ♫.
7. Finally, play the entire piece, omitting both ♫ and ♩.

Use in the Church Choir

The Orff Schulwerk is generally perceived as "schoolwork," the business of music educators in the classroom. Transplanting the techniques and musical style to the worship service, however, poses no great problems. Beyond the novelty and charm of the instrumental aspect of the approach, the function of the children's choir in the church service is the same: to provide a special dimension to the act of corporate worship. Artistic performance in the totality of singing, speech, instruments, and movement combined with attitudes of worship will ensure that the Orff choir is more than a cute adornment to an otherwise routine service.

Congregations that are accepting of experimentation in worship will likely welcome the vitality and genuine beauty that Orff settings (including speech, movement, and/or instruments as well as singing) have to offer. Children engaged in music in such compelling ways can be a most inspirational sight as well and rejuvenating to the worshiper for whom the experience has become pretty predictable.

Short responsorial portions of the service are enhanced by Orff arrangements, such as Psalm responses or other litanies offered by the congregation. (See Boshkoff arrangement in Chapter 5.) The children may sing the verses, and instruments may be used with verses or responses or both. Introits and benedictions are also suitable for such participation by children with instruments, as are anthems and carols.

The following example uses light texture and metal instruments to support the innocent quality of a carol for young children.

Example 4.43

Manger Carol

Words and music
S. W. M.

2. Behold the wise men from afar
   Above the manger shines a star.
   Alleluia! Alleluia!

3. The shepherds on the starlit hill
   Beyond the manger seek him still.
   Alleluia! Alleluia!

4. "Noel, Noel," the children sing,
   Within the manger to the king.
   Alleluia! Alleluia!

Form: Introduction = 4 bars accompaniment

Verse 1
 Interlude
 Verse 2
  etc.
 Coda

Perhaps a more important consideration is the unique value of the Orff Schulwerk to the children themselves. We have already described the musical development that can occur through such experiences, but what of the growth of the spirit? Choirs exist for children, not the reverse. There is within music the power to portray feelings and also to express feelings. Thus musical experiences may relate to life experience itself and specifically to the social, emotional, and religious growth of children. The Schulwerk, then, makes no preposterous claims upon these areas of development. The distinctive characteristics of Orff music experiences, however, do combine to contribute with unusual success to the comprehensive development of the child. The body, the mind, and the spirit are simultaneously involved in each musical event, not passively but directly. The act of worship becomes authentic and personal for the child who is an active participant in its expression. God continues the process of creation through the creative efforts of children.

Creativity, often lauded but seldom understood and cultivated, is regarded by many as an extraordinary artistic capacity with which some few people are mysteriously endowed. Unfortunately, such a view disregards any responsibility to seek and develop creative instincts among ordinary folk. The Schulwerk, being an approach that prizes and nurtures the inventiveness believed to be natural to children, thereby affirms the ongoing creation of God.

The exclusiveness sometimes attached to the field of music is avoided in the Orff classroom. Because of its inherent flexibility, the process makes possible the successful participation of every child, at some level and in some aspect. An accompaniment pattern can be altered to match the ability of an individual child without forfeiting the overall musical integrity; the poor singer may be very comfortable with speech or movement or instruments.

Finally, a respect for childhood is evident in the Schulwerk, as teaching strategies capitalize upon those ways of making music that are natural and familiar. The atmosphere of acceptance and pleasure builds self-esteem, confidence, and awareness of diverse points of view.

The question invariably arises "How do we do all this in a one-hour rehearsal?" This is a legitimate point, given the volunteer nature of choirs, infrequent rehearsals, and the usual performance responsibilities.

The ideal solution is to integrate Orff activities into as many aspects of the rehearsal as possible, although there will undoubtedly be warm-ups and games that are useful in themselves.

Hymns and anthems may be approached through rhythmic preparation, movement, or speech. Vocal warm-ups and reading exercises are likely to be more beneficial if related to music to be learned, rather than isolated drills apart from any real musical context.

Rehearsals that have individual focus as well as a function with a long-range plan tend to be more efficient. Obviously, not all musical concepts can be covered in each session, but a haphazard, hit-or-miss approach will result in only fragmented learning unlikely to carry over to other musical contexts. What the musical concepts will be for a given rehearsal may be determined in part by the problems presented in the hymns and anthems to be learned. Other aspects may be chosen arbitrarily by the director to ensure that overall musical competence is developed.

A director who is knowledgeable about the goals and techniques of the Orff Schulwerk will find ways not only to introduce new material and teach concepts in an Orff manner but also to enhance conventional settings. Such "tampering" assumes, to be sure, a respect for the character and style of the music, as well as for the unique elemental Orff sound. Some song material does not lend itself to this orchestral style. The judicious use of instruments and interpretive movement or dance, especially with choral speech, can add vitality, color, and excitement to some materials.

The following example uses a B section, an introduction, and a coda, adding a few Orff instruments, to extend the piece. Christmas words may be substituted as indicated.

Example 4.44

On This Happy Easter

Grace S. Tower

V. Earle Copes

Introduction and Coda:

The director who wishes to incorporate elements of the Orff Schulwerk into the choir rehearsal will find it essential to plan meticulously and talk little; the most efficient rehearsals are carefully sequenced and keep the children actively involved as much as possible. The director may then find that more material is covered, pacing improves, interest increases, and behavior problems are minimized.

Summary

The Orff Schulwerk is a way of experiencing music in the most natural (active, integrated) fashion and in an environment of creative play. It is based on the philosophy that all children will respond positively to music when taught in ways that relate to their developmental levels. Work and play are synthesized, with rhythm, movement, and melody as the core ingredients, and the children are encouraged to take risks in terms of their own musical ideas. The teacher's role is to stimulate the exploratory process and to guide the learners into higher levels of musical experimentation and artistry. Such competencies lead to pleasure and confidence in future experiences in the art, self-esteem through supportive relationships within the group, and the intellectual, motor, and aesthetic growth to which music activities naturally contribute.

CHAPTER 5

Preparing for the Choir's Year

"Everything depends on the leader."
—ZOLTÁN KODÁLY

Most though not all of what succeeds in a rehearsal is a result of what goes into its preparation. Just as a smooth and enjoyable dinner party depends in large measure upon planning and foresight, a productive rehearsal is born of preparation well in advance of the event itself. Such a statement is not to negate the inevitable spontaneous moments of joy and excitement that result from the creative interaction of teacher and children. Indeed, rehearsal rigidity and predictability are deadly to choir morale and may actually impede the learning process.

The point is that there are a number of organizational and musical tasks that, if done before the choir season begins, prevent stressful conflicts and last-minute panic. Most of the considerations add up to good administration of time and resources. These may be categorized as organizational tasks and musical tasks.

ORGANIZATIONAL TASKS

Determine Needs

The director's first job, especially if the choir program is a new one, is to assess the needs of the program in general and each choir in particular. How many children are expected? What are their ages? What schools do they attend? Where do they live? What age groupings are anticipated, resulting in what size ensembles? What, then, are the expected needs in rehearsal space and support personnel? Will there be accompanists or other assistants? How much will it cost?

A review and clarification of choir goals is valuable at this stage. If education in musicianship is a primary focus, certain needs (space, materials, equipment) will emerge. Heavy performance responsibilities dictate other needs, especially in regard to musical materials. If choir workbooks are used, much preparation will be involved.

A projected budget closely follows an assessment of needs, and is based on goals for the year and the resources deemed necessary to reach them. Suggested budget items are listed later in this chapter. At this point it need only be said that budget requests which are directly related to mutually-perceived goals and which are presented in advance of the choir season are more likely to be favorably received.

Select a Theme

Many directors like to provide a theme, a focus, for the choir season. This idea was explored in Chapter 1, page 8. A theme often suggests a slogan and a logo that may be used in all correspondence and publicity, and rehearsal rooms may be decorated according to this chosen theme. Such devices capitalize upon imagery and visual impact.[1]

Devise an Award System

Since the children's church choir is generally perceived as a service activity, some kind of award system can provide additional incentive. While the work of the choir is designed to educate and to provide unique service opportunities for the children, extrinsic rewards are not necessarily in contradiction to this perception. Unless the award system is overemphasized or unfairly administered, it can provide a special kind of morale boost. Awards are of two kinds: some kind of recognition of service, given to all choristers; and special awards to those who meet certain standards of achievement. Many directors choose to provide both types of recognition. Suggestions for a recognition service are found in Chapter 8, page 197.

Achievement or merit awards are usually presented in some kind of end-of-the-year recognition service at Sunday worship or, if the choirs are many, at a special family event. The awards may take many forms:

1. a certificate of achievement, framed or unframed
2. a pin
3. a cross pendant
4. a personal hymnal

---

[1] For clever uses of bulletin board space, see Bonnie Jean Early, "See What I Mean?" *Choristers Guild Letters,* March 1987, 182–83.

Suitable certificates and jewelry are available from the Choristers Guild and the Royal School of Church Music, as well as some denominational bookstores (see Appendix C). Some directors have the jewelry returned and reawarded, thus limiting expense to the initial purchase cost.

The basis for making achievement awards must be objective, reasonable, and clearly stated at the beginning. Nebulous standards open to debate and negotiation are counterproductive to healthy morale; and intricate, detailed requirements call for too much bookkeeping and may become too legalistic to be worth the effort. Again, the most desirable reward for singing in any church choir, the satisfaction generated through personal service and through music itself, should not be minimized. What, then, are some of the bases for merit awards?

1. Choir attendance. A minimum expectation needs to be stated; performances are included as well as rehearsals. Extra, or unscheduled, events may or may not be a part of this expectation but need to be anticipated. Most directors prefer that the attendance requirement, once set, be nonnegotiable, as determining which absences are "excused" becomes subjective and thus fosters ill will.

2. Church-school attendance. Some directors, wishing to reinforce the overall educational emphasis of the choir program, include this area of achievement. However, the extra record-keeping may become tiresome.

3. Some evidence of musical growth, such as learning all music from memory, memorizing a stated number of hymns, or good singing habits.

4. Excellent deportment. This is somewhat subjective and may be difficult to assess, but certainly children whose behavior is generally disruptive would not be eligible for awards.

5. Workbook care. Workbooks shall be kept clean and neat and any work sheets completed. They are to be brought to each rehearsal.

6. Recruitment. Bringing a new chorister may be a part of the merit system, provided the child remains with the choir for a specified period of time.

Aside from merit awards, regular "perks" such as stickers, parties, singing engagements outside the normal church service, and festivals are all morale boosters. Once a system of recognition of all the types described has been established, the incentive for commitment to choir goals increases. Children who witness an ongoing custom of awards for service and achievement want to participate themselves.

Determine Performance Schedule

The director should attempt to schedule all singing responsibilities for as much of the year as possible before the singing season begins. Parents especially appreciate this consideration, but it also makes possible better coordination among all programs of the church. This coordination in turn results in better attendance at all functions.

From the director's standpoint, such advance information helps maintain the education-performance balance. Furthermore, the need for anthems and other materials that must be selected and ordered will be projected more accurately.

Meet with Choir Sponsors or Assistants

Undoubtedly the music director will enlist the aid of assistants of some kind, especially if there are several choirs or if the choir itself is large. Sharing responsibilities also tends to extend interest beyond the persons directly involved in music preparation (director, accompanist, and children). Ordinarily these assistants are chosen from family members of choristers or from older students with an interest in such activities. High school or college choir singers sometimes enjoy helping with the younger choirs. The specific duties of volunteer assistants were suggested in Chapter 1, page 12. Meeting with these individuals before the choir season gets underway is a good time to interpret goals; prepare the schedule of rehearsals, performances, and other events; and assign duties to the assistants. Such a support system can be invaluable to the director throughout the year.

Find Suitable Rehearsal Space

Normally, the sanctuary is not a satisfactory rehearsal area, except just prior to a performance. Generally speaking, younger choirs require more open space for movement activities than do the older ensembles. Physical conditions are very important, and bright attractive rooms that reflect children's interests make the best learning environment. Adequate lighting, comfortable seating (which varies with the age of the children), and space for visual aids all pay off in musical results as well as behavior.

The arrangement of the rehearsal space can take several forms, depending again upon the functions of the individual choir, the ages of the children, and the personal style of the director. Figures 5.2–5.5 show some possibilities.

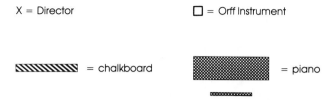

X = Director   □ = Orff Instrument

▨▨▨▨▨ = chalkboard   ▨▨▨▨▨▨ = piano

Figure 5.1. Legend for Figures 5.2–5.5.

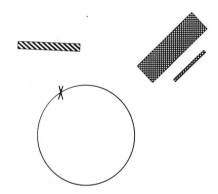

Figure 5.2. Preschool choir, with children seated on the floor (on carpet squares).

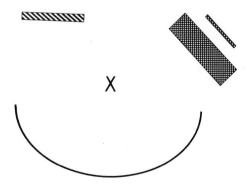

Figure 5.3. Small older choir, with regular accompanist.

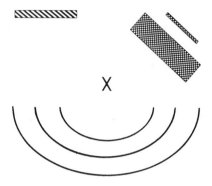

Figure 5.4. Larger older choir, with regular accompanist.

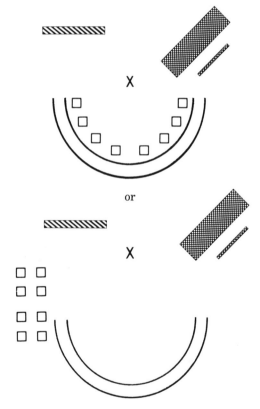

Figure 5.5. Choir that also uses Orff instruments.

Figure 5.6. Entire choir in semicircle arrangement with Orff instruments.

The semicircular arrangement is preferred because it enables the children to hear each other and because it seems less rigid and formal than straight rows.

Check Equipment

Anticipating choral needs includes a variety of equipment, instrumental and otherwise. A sturdy adjustable music stand, storage space for music, visual aids, choir robes, and Orff instruments are all obvious essentials. Storage space is especially important if rehearsals are held in multipurpose rooms. In this event, arrangements must be made regarding use of bulletin boards and wall space as well as the room itself.

A portable chalkboard is indispensable if there is not a chalkboard in a convenient location. Magnetic boards, flannel boards, and pocket charts (used by elementary classroom teachers and available at school supply stores) are useful to supplement wall boards. Pacing of a rehearsal can be seriously disrupted if visual aids are not within easy reach.

A well-tuned piano is essential. Church pianos are notorious for their abuse and disrepair, but it is counterproductive to positive musical experiences to work with an inadequate instrument. Insist on this provision.

Prepare Workbooks or Folders

Children need something tangible to focus their attention on choir activities. At the very least they need folders in which to keep music in order.

Many directors like to use workbooks of some sort, full of activities, puzzles, words to hymns and anthems (copyright permitting), study sheets, prayers, and the like. Much of this must be designed, duplicated, and put into loose-leaf binders or folders before the season gets underway (see chapter appendix for sample worksheets). They are connecting links to an infrequent (or so it seems to the child) experience that they can take home and share with the family. Giving out new materials at regular intervals is better than distributing the entire workbook early in the year. Stickers may be added to certain pages as little rewards for a job well done. In spite of the effort required for preparing them, workbooks add greatly to teaching effectiveness and choir morale.

Donita Banks lists numerous uses for workbooks, including all learning and organizational materials for the year.[2] Learning materials include puzzles, cartoons, musical activities, instrument charts, Scripture readings, and hymn studies. Organizational materials include an awards system page, information for parents, a calendar, a list of choristers, and an attendance chart. Workbooks are organized and musical materials selected with a yearly theme in mind, such as (1) meaning of the worship service, (2) world missions and songs, (3) celebrations, (4) study of Moses, (5) parables.

MUSICAL TASKS

Establish Goals

While the broad purpose and general goals of the choir program are best developed cooperatively, purely musical objectives are usually the responsibility of the director, who will be working directly with the choristers. Expectations that are challenging but commensurate with the developmental levels of the children were analyzed at length in Chapter 3. Establishing and verbalizing these musical goals gives direction and focus to the leader and facilitates planning for sequence and growth.

Select Materials

Often regarded as the most time-consuming task, the selection of suitable musical materials indeed requires much thought and sensitivity to the

---

[2]Donita Banks, "Learning Unlimited," *Choristers Guild Letters,* March 1986, 157.

needs and capabilities of the singers. Once again, the basic function of the choir program will dictate in part the amount and nature of the music to be learned. Complete resources of the church must be taken into account, especially with regard to the accompaniments. Younger choirs will rely less upon anthem materials and thereby incur less expense in this area. Multiple copies of numbers of anthems constitute a considerable expenditure, so selections must be carefully made. Insofar as possible, all musical materials should be made in advance of the choir season for budgetary reasons, if none other.

It is helpful to consult the lectionary and/or persons responsible for planning worship services. The director will also keep in mind the various seasons, festivals, and other special events observed by the congregation. This awareness will ensure that the choral program contributes to the growth of the children as participating church members. There are several categories of musical materials to be included in a balanced choir program.

Hymns

Developing a broad repertoire of hymns begins in childhood. Many adults have only a limited perspective of Judeo-Christian hymnody and, unfortunately, are not always eager to expand their knowledge. An appreciation of the great heritage of hymns, ancient and modern, is a wonderful asset to an individual and to a congregation. The choir is the logical place for such appreciation to take root, for the children are open-minded and curious about all kinds of musical expression. A systematic study of hymns may take two forms: regular rehearsing of hymns to be used in worship services, and hymns to be studied in depth during the choir season. The latter category suggests workbook pages that give information about the author and the source of the music, interpretation of the text, structure of the melody, and relationship of the text to the child's religious life. Many delightful hymn pages are available from the Choristers Guild. Care should be taken as to quality of the text and music and appropriateness of the hymn for the children involved. Such a statement does not imply childish hymns but, rather, the great, standard hymns that will likely be a part of the child's lifelong church experience but within general comprehension. See chapter appendix for examples of hymn study pages.

Other Worship Materials

The choir rehearsal is the ideal time to train children in liturgical music. Some of the responses and doxologies they can learn to sing themselves; others can be introduced and explained.

Example below:

Example 5.1

PSALM 136

Psalm response: "Give thanks to the Lord, for He is good;
For His love endures forever."

Ruth Boshkoff

O give thanks to the Lord _ for

He __ is good   for his   love __ en - dures _ for - ev - er. __

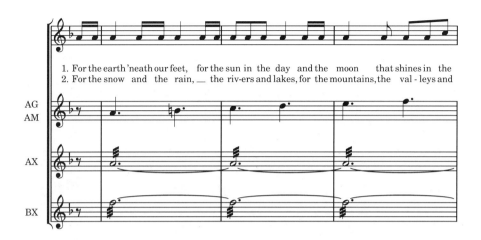

The refrain should be sung first by the cantor and repeated by the congregation. Thus the form is A A B A B A Coda.

The function of the organ prelude and postlude can be clarified. Melodies for short blessings and Scripture sentences may be created by the choristers themselves, given an environment and structure conducive to such a task. Table blessings and bedtime prayers for use at home, and included in choir workbooks, may be a part of the choir repertoire. Likewise, special settings for use in rehearsal are helpful.

Example 5.2

A PRAYER FOR REHEARSAL

S. W. M.

Thank _ you, God, for mu - sic, A gift _ for us to share, With

grate - ful hearts we sing your praise, and of - fer you _ this

prayer. A - men, A - men.

Criteria for Anthems

Anthems for use in worship form the nucleus of most choral repertoire. Much time must be devoted to examining music in order to find literature that will meet vocal and spiritual standards and also be within the capabilities of the musicians. There are three considerations (aside from cost) that govern the selection of anthems: text, vocal score, and accompaniment. The outline of children's personal and musical characteristics at various ages provided in Chapter 3 may be helpful in making appropriate choices. Criteria given here are more general and apply specifically to anthems.

1. Text

- Can the children understand its general meaning?
- Is it relatively free of symbolic language?
- Will the children relate to the subject matter?
- Are words and music compatible in meter and character?
- Is it theologically sound?
- Does it have poetic merit?
- Is it childlike without being condescending?

2. Vocal Score

- Is the tessitura suitable, so as to encourage beautiful singing without strain or use of chest voice?
- Is it simple but beautiful and appealing?
- Are the phrases singable in one breath?
- Is it relatively free of difficult intervals?
- Does it have musical merit?

3. Accompaniment

- Is it within the capabilities of the accompanist?
- Does it call for other instruments not readily available?
- Will it require extensive alterations to be usable?
- Is it free of trite harmonic and rhythmic clichés?
- Is the texture light but supportive of children's voices?
- Is it musically interesting on its own without confusing the singer?

Since anthems are the only music most of the congregation will ever hear the children sing, naturally they should be chosen carefully to reflect the best in the children as well as for their intrinsic value.

Fun Songs and Educational Materials

Every rehearsal should contain short, simple songs and games for warm-ups and change of pace, or to reinforce some specific musical skill. Typically, directors like to begin and end rehearsals with such informal material, but young bodies and minds often need reviving at other times as well. After a long period of sitting, or concentrating on some difficult music, everybody benefits from a quick change of pace. Specific vocalises or exercises to prepare for the next piece on the agenda are most relevant in that context.

Since singing is a physical activity that makes demands on the entire body, an active warm-up at the beginning of rehearsal is fun and energizing.

Example 5.3

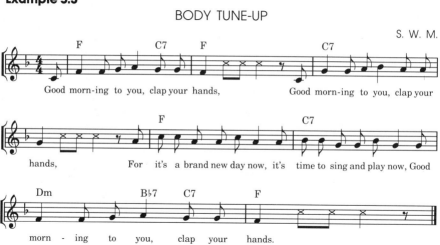

This is a cumulative action song. Verse two:

> Good morning to you, stamp your feet . . .
> Action: stamp ♪♪♩, then clap ♪♪♩ and so on throughout the verse.

3: Snap your fingers (actions: snap, then stamp, then clap . . .)

4. Pat your knees . . .

5. Say "hallelu" . . .

6. Wave goodbye . . .

The song may be altered for afternoon use:

> A good day to you . . .
> For it's a happy day now . . .

Or evening:

> Good evening to you . . .

Musical concepts are best taught in ways that actively involve the children. Usually this approach employs movement, speech, visual aids, manipulation of objects, or combinations of these.

Musical concept: relative note values ♩ ♩ ♫

Movement

- Establish a ♩ beat on a drum.
- Children create their own movements to match (shrug shoulders, bounce in place, walk); share these ideas.
- Change to ♩, then ♫, creating appropriate movements for each.
- Practice going from one to the other; change movements each time; try other people's movement ideas.
- Select instruments to represent each sound (♩ = something that sustains; ♩ = something fairly heavy; ♫ = something light and crisp).
- Let the instruments dictate the movement: respond in movement to the sounds that are heard.
- Combine two or more (maintaining a common pulse), children choose one, or divide class into groups for each note value.

Visuals

- Show rhythmic symbols for ♩ ♩ ♫.
- Practice clapping each; speaking the syllables helps (♩ = ta-a; ♩ = ta; ♫ = ti ti).
- Add quarter rest 𝄽 (say "sh" or make a silent motion).
- Put notes together in combinations, with speech patterns if desired:
  Job = ♩   David = ♩♩   Jeremiah = ♫ ♫

Speech

- Learn the verse "Be ye kind, one to another."
- Speak rhythmically: 1) ♩ ♩ | 2) ♩ | ♩ ♫ | ♩ ♩ ‖

- Speak in canon, clap in canon.
- Choose the rhythmic symbols for each word and write them on the board.
- Play a bordun on a bass metallophone or soft chord patterns on guitar or piano.

Example 5.4

- Children make up melodies for the text (F pentatonic is a good structure).

Example 5.5

- Notate some of these on the staff, for example:

Example 5.6

- Compare the rhythmic setting with the melodic one: how are they different? how are they the same?

For a ready, fast method of focusing attention, relaxing the body, or sharpening listening skills, nothing works better than a few rhythmic echoes. Four beat patterns clapped or patsched

♩♫♩♩ (echo)

♪♩♪♩𝄽 (echo)

demand immediate feedback and can bring a group to attention subtly, effortlessly, and quicker than any other method.

Work with the Accompanist

Unless the choir director also does the accompanying, there needs to be communication before the rehearsal gets under way. The accompanist needs advance notice of tempi, dynamics, and any modifications in the score, especially if transposition is involved. Most accompanists prefer not to go into a rehearsal without having had time to prepare. The notion that it doesn't matter so much for children's choirs is an insidious one and is disrespectful of the children. Not only is such consultation only fair and courteous, it makes for more efficient rehearsing. Problem spots can be identified early and perhaps minimized, and the accompanist is better able to adjust the keyboard part as needed to support the singers. This ability is especially valuable in the early stages of learning an anthem.

The accompanist needs to know what teaching strategies will involve the piano: vocalises, movement activities, fun songs that may require improvised accompaniments. Being familiar with the director's style and techniques makes for better rehearsing and fewer lags in the pacing. When everyone is comfortable and relaxed, the musical results will improve and morale will be good. A good accompanist—sensitive, supportive and able to anticipate musical problems—is a pearl of great price. The wise director will cultivate a good relationship and give due recognition to this valuable assistant. Note: If the person accompanying the children in performance is someone other than the rehearsal pianist, then that person deserves the same advance consideration.

Finally, if other instruments are called for in the accompaniment, those players need to be identified and scheduled well in advance. This is particularly important at Christmas and Easter, when instrumentalists are in greater demand.

Analyze the Music

No doubt some analysis of the music takes place in the selection process, as the director considers what will or will not work in a given piece. Matching materials with one's resources is a finely developed skill that depends in part on experience but also on anticipating success or failure through intelligent analysis of the score.

Once a piece has been chosen, the director needs to become thoroughly familiar with all aspects of it and perhaps memorize it. A director who is overly dependent on the score is at a great disadvantage, especially with children, who rely heavily on eye contact and facial expression for direction. Problems in the music can be anticipated and minimized by advance study, and any alterations in the score can be made early and not have to be corrected later. This subject is explored fully in Chapter 7.

BUDGET

Nobody likes to deal with budgets because they usually have to be cut. Most churches have limits to which all programs, however valuable and popular, must adhere. The choral program is no exception, and the director will want to explore sources of revenue and ways to economize. Duplicating music illegally is not recommended as a way of saving money, even though the cost of multiple scores is considerable.

At this point, let us list some areas of expense that may need to be projected and budgeted. Even if cuts must be made, church finance committees are likely to look kindly upon requests that are responsible and well thought out.

1. *Salaries, honoraria.* Even if the musical leadership is volunteer, there may be occasions for employing an instrumentalist or a guest conductor. Appropriate honoraria should be projected.

2. *Music.* Multiple copies of anthems will incur the greatest expense. Sometimes collections are practical and cost-efficient if most of the music is immediately usable.

    Some songs can be taught by rote, especially with young choirs, and the church's hymnal is a rich and accessible source of suitable material. Anthem collections and children's hymnals are listed in Appendix B.

    A reasonably accurate projection of music expenditures is possible after tentative selections are made for the year. Of course, once the choral program is well established, the music library increases, and subsequent additions incur less expense.

3. *Duplicating costs.* If materials for workbooks and programs for special events are extensive, duplicating costs are significant. Even if these services are provided by the church, some anticipated expenditure is appropriate.

4. *Other supplies.* An active program for even one children's choir will no doubt require posters and other visual aids, postcards, workbooks and/or folders for music, and awards (pins, certificates, and the like). Bulletin boards, chalkboards, and teaching equipment should be considered.

5. *Vestments.* No doubt the singers may require vestments or robes of some kind for use in worship services. Newly organized choirs can expect a sizable outlay of funds in this category, whether the robes are purchased or made by volunteer seamstresses. Thereafter, cleaning bills must be projected.

6. *Instruments.* Assuming there is already a satisfactory accompanying keyboard instrument for rehearsals and services, there may be interest in building a supply of instruments that the children them-

selves may play. Simple percussion instruments (enough for each child to play) are indispensable with young choirs. Older ones will be charmed with barred percussion for accompanying or improvisation. Orff instruments of this variety were described on page 75. While the full range of these instruments makes a versatile and enchanting ensemble, they may be purchased gradually. A list of suppliers may be found in Appendix C. A suggested order of purchase in each category follows:

Percussion

triangle or finger cymbals (for color in arrangements)

rhythm sticks (inexpensive and useful for developing musicianship)

four or five hand drums of two or three sizes (for orchestrations and motor development)

tambourine (for orchestrations and motor development)

wood blocks or temple blocks (for color)

Barred

alto xylophone (versatile)

soprano and alto glockenspiels (for color)

bass xylophone (foundation for orchestrations)

alto metallophone (fill in the ranges)

soprano xylophone (not resonant; more than one may be required)

soprano metallophone (same pitch as alto glockenspiel)

bass metallophone (wonderful sound but the least versatile)

Other

Orff timpani or Roto Tom (versatile and exciting)

maracas (for color)

brass chime bar or bell tree (magical for color)

suspended cymbal (for color)

7. *Social.* Unless parties and refreshments on special occasions are financed by contributions for that purpose, such expenses will need to be a budget item. However, parents are often willing to donate food and other supplies for social events.

SUMMARY

The analogy to a dinner party, made at the beginning of this chapter, is still valid. The menu must be selected, the guests contacted, all other expenses projected, and the grocery list completed before the actual cooking gets underway. If the preparation has been thorough, the party itself will seem effortless and guests will comment on the relaxed atmosphere.

Likewise, the director who plans and consults and anticipates will realize a payoff in terms of morale and productivity. Any unexpected problems that then occur will not seem insurmountable, and the choral experience will be a joyous one for director and choristers alike.

Joyful, Joyful, We Adore Thee

The tune for this hymn was written by a very famous composer, Ludwig van Beethoven. He was born in Bonn, Germany, and began studying music at the age of 4. When he was 11 he published his first works. As a young man he settled in Vienna and gained fame there both as a pianist and composer. He began to lose his hearing when only 27 and was completely deaf at the age of 39. He overcame this handicap and wrote 9 symphonies, 32 piano sonatas, 5 piano concertos, and 16 string quartets.

Many of you are probably familiar with the beginning of Beethoven's Fifth Symphony. The tune for "Joyful, Joyful, We Adore Thee" was written for the finale, or ending, of his Ninth Symphony. It is called the "Choral Symphony" because it is the only Beethoven symphony that has singing in it.

The Ninth Symphony was first performed on May 7, 1824. The audience applauded loudly at the end of the performance, but Beethoven did not turn around to bow because he could not hear it. One of the singers touched his sleeve and pointed to the audience, so Beethoven turned around and saw the people clapping and waving hats and handkerchiefs. It was then that he realized that his symphony was a success, so he bowed to the audience.

Beethoven wanted to compose a setting of Schiller's "Ode to Joy" for a long time. He tried many times to find just the right way. The words of Schiller's poem talk about the universal brotherhood of man through joy and the fact that this love for each other is based in the love of our heavenly father. The words in our hymnal were written by Henry van Dyke, but they talk about the same things. Find some of the lines of the hymn that talk about loving each other. Write them on the lines below.

_____

_____

_____

_____

_____

—Worksheet by Ellen Koziel, used by permission

Joyful, Joyful, We Adore Thee

Fill in the missing words to the hymn. Take the letters that are circled and write them at the bottom of the page to find out the composer of this hymn tune!

1. Joyful, joyful, we [ ] Thee,

   God of glory, Lord of [ ],

   Hearts unfold like flowers [ ] Thee,

   Opening to the sun [ ].

   [ ] the clouds of sin and sadness,

   Drive the dark of [ ] away,

   Giver of immortal [ ],

   Fill us with the [ ] of day.

2. All Thy works with [ ] surround Thee,

   Earth and heaven reflect Thy rays,

   Stars and angels [ ] around Thee,

   Center of unbroken praise.

   Field and forest, [ ] and mountain,

   Flowery meadow, flashing [ ],

   Chanting bird and flowing [ ],

   Call us to rejoice in Thee.

   [ ][ ][ ][ ][ ][ ][ ][ ]

—Ellen Koziel, used by permission

All Creatures of Our God and King

St. Francis of Assisi
Tr. W. H. Draper

Lasst uns erfreuen, 1623
Arr. & Harm. by
R. V. Williams, 1872–1958

ST. FRANCIS OF ASSISI

The words to this pleasant _____ were written by a

_____ known as St. Francis of Assisi. Assisi is a little _____

in _____. St. Francis spent his last days living at a convent called

St. Damian, just outside Assisi, where the nuns known as _____

looked after him when he came there ill, blind, and lonely. St. Francis

loved the simple things of life, all of _____ creation, and he had a

special love for all the _____. St. Francis was a _____ man

and would say "a single _____ is enough to drive away many

_____." The _____ for this famous hymn of praise comes

from 17th-century Germany. As we sing these words that St. Francis

wrote, think how happy he was to write praising God for all the things

and animals He made for us to enjoy. Sing joyfully the "Alleluia."

Missing words from the story

shadows	God's	melody	town	Italy	animals
hymn	Poor Clares	monk	happy	sunbeam	

—Charlotte Kronschnabel, used by permission

127

EARTH AND ALL STARS

(Written in 1968)

Words by:
(H. Brokering)

Music by:
(David Johnson)

In our church, we usually __(kneel)__ to pray, __(stand)__ to praise, and __(sit)__ when we are being taught (during the lessons and the sermon). A hymn is a song of praise to God and is usually sung standing.

God created many different types of people who praise him in many different ways. Some people write poetry, some paint pictures, and some compose or perform music to the glory of God. Can you think of several ways that you might praise God in your everyday life?

_____

_____

The Psalms tell about how people praised God many years ago: with timbrel and dance, lute and harp, strings and loud crashing cymbals. This hymn is a modern way to praise God. See if you can match the six verses to these sentences.

Verse __(3)__ Musicians might use these instruments to praise God.

Verse __(5)__ Students and teachers can praise God at school, too.

Verse __(2)__ It doesn't matter what season it is, or what the weather is like. We can praise God all year long!

Verse __(4)__ Even construction workers can use their tools to praise.

Verse __(1)__ Let all the universe praise God!

Verse __(6)__ Families and congregation praise God with their words.

Try to answer these musical questions about this hymn. Underline the correct answer or fill in the blank.

- There are two sections to this hymn. Another name for the B section is (verse, refrain).

- If hymns used meter signatures, this hymn would be in (3, 4).

- The name of this hymn is ("Praise to God," "Earth and All Stars").

- The composer wanted to make several words very important. He did this by using 4 ♩'s for one syllable. Name the two words.

_____ and _____

—Debbie Clifton, used by permission

Hidden Treasure

It is time to learn about the hymn " __6_ __1_ _14_ __9_ _14_ __9_ __2_ _11_

__5_ _12_ __6_ __1_ _26_ __8_ __9_ _17_ __7_ __8_ _21_ __4_ ." The words to this hymn

were written by __2_ _12_ _21_ __6_ _13_ _14_ _26_ __4_ . _13_ _12_ _13_ _16_ __7_

_16_ _20_ . The tune was written by __5_ __8_ _12_ _23_ _20_ _21_ _14_ _23_ _21_ .

__9_ __1_ _26_ __3_ __3_ _12_ __8_ __4_ . Can you find this hymn in your hymnal?
Find where these names are located.

This is a hymn of praise for God's _16_ __8_ _26_ _12_ __6_ _14_ __7_ _23_ . God

has created all of _23_ _12_ __6_ _18_ __8_ _26_ to praise Him. We can enjoy the

praise of God's creation, but we must _21_ _14_ __9_ __6_ _26_ _23_ . God also

wants us to recognize His greatness by __9_ _26_ _26_ _14_ _23_ _25_ His crea-

tion. All the beautiful things __4_ _26_ _16_ _21_ _12_ __8_ _26_ their

__2_ _12_ _20_ _26_ __8_ __9_ praise.

Code

1	2	3	4	5	6	7	8	9	10	11	12	13
H	M	P	D	F	T	O	R	S	X	Y	A	B

14	15	16	17	18	19	20	21	22	23	24	25	26
I	J	C	W	U	V	K	L	Z	N	Q	G	E

There are at least twenty things in this hymn that God has created. Can you find them all (vertical, horizontal, and backward)?

```
R  W  O  D  I  G  H  E  A  R  E  V  C  C  O  E
T  O  M  X  B  P  Q  O  C  U  E  I  A  L  E  H
R  W  O  A  I  J  G  H  E  S  W  O  R  L  D  E
E  A  R  S  R  K  C  E  L  T  E  U  O  X  V  R
E  T  N  Y  D  O  E  R  E  L  J  K  L  L  W  A
S  W  I  T  S  W  M  U  S  I  C  D  S  K  O  M
N  B  N  X  C  R  W  T  Z  N  G  H  P  E  N  O
T  D  G  R  E  E  G  A  E  G  H  O  H  P  D  N
S  E  L  I  L  Y  R  N  N  G  C  L  E  X  E  E
E  G  I  H  E  S  K  C  O  R  S  O  R  C  R  V
A  X  G  O  E  I  O  S  N  A  E  O  E  E  S  A
S  R  H  T  O  S  K  I  E  S  P  I  O  N  M  E
R  T  T  H  O  U  G  H  T  S  C  E  A  R  T  H
```

—Terry Tankersley, used by permission

CHAPTER 6

Working with the Child's Voice

"The first month of a nightingale's life determines its fate."
—SHINICHI SUZUKI

The monumental significance of positive early experiences with music has been discussed in previous chapters of this book. The key words in the above sentence are "positive," "early," and "experiences." Attitudes formed about music and one's relationships to it often persist for life. Children who are told, however subtly, that they are unmusical, tend to believe it and grow up to be "unmusical" adults, apologetic or negative about music. The second key word, "early," tells us that the most important learnings, the ones that stay with us, occur early in life. Thus, capitalizing upon the child's instinctive love for all things musical is the essence of early musical training. The fun of exploring sounds and movement is natural to the child and builds a foundation for later, more formal "experiences"—the third key word. While structured lessons and classes have a place in musical development, music education does not always take the form of conscious instruction.

Few people would recommend private voice lessons for a six-year-old or even an eleven-year-old. A child this young is not physiologically or psychologically ready for such intensive study. However, young children need many experiences in vocal play and singing to develop an awareness of their voices and what it feels like to sing in tune with others. The teacher, of course, should always present a good model of tone quality and intonation. By middle elementary years, children may be taught the physiological aspects of singing and basic concepts about posture, breathing, and diction while refining the head voice quality. Good habits at this stage not only produce more musical performances but also protect the child against vocal damage.

VOCAL PRINCIPLES AND TECHNIQUES

The Vocal Mechanism

Singing is an action of the whole body as well as the mind. Proper singing requires energy and exertion, muscle control, and stamina, developed gradually through the practice of good habits. Children's choir directors must understand the singing mechanism and be able to help children establish vocal health:

> The idea that singing is a psychomotor skill is certainly not a new one, but its serious implications have been overlooked far too long in regard to children learning to sing. The process of singing is complex, requiring many psychomotor coordinations . . . Yet many teachers of children's singing seem to expect that coordination of the singing voice will happen automatically.[1]

Even the basic ability to match pitch is perceived by some to be directly related to coordination of the vocal mechanism as much as a function of aural discrimination. In any case, we acknowledge the essential physiological aspect of singing and the necessity to train the body to make proper use of this capacity.

Children may be taught to regard their singing voice as a musical instrument that is distinctive and capable of producing a variety of beautiful sounds. It is thus worthy of respect and proper care. Just as a clarinet or a trumpet has parts that function together to produce tones, the vocal mechanism is a coordination of body parts.

Since air is necessary for singing, the lungs act as a generator, producing a stream of air that must pass between the vocal folds. These folds open for breathing and close and vibrate for phonation (tone production). For the tone to have character and carrying power, it depends upon a resonating space (compare to the hollow box beneath the xylophone or that of a guitar or violin). The human voice finds resonance in the larynx, the pharynx, the mouth, and the nasal cavity. The shape of these cavities may be modified by changes in the shape of the mouth, position of the jaw, and movement of the tongue. The resonating chamber is also affected by congestion from an infection or allergic reaction. This is easily demonstrated to the children by having them hold their noses as they speak or sing.

---

[1]Kenneth H. Phillips, "Training the Child Voice," *Music Educators Journal,* December 1985, 22.

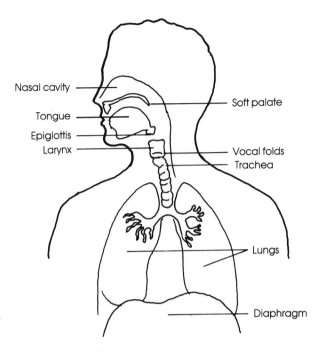

Figure 6.1. Vocal tract with resonating cavities.

The act of singing is not complete, however, without articulation. The mouth (lips, tongue, jaw, teeth) is the source of articulation, with consonants being the vehicle. Temporary interruptions of the air stream, which consonants produce, give vitality and meaning to the sung text. Articulation problems, which form the most common type of speech disorders among school-age children, are often found among singers as well. The function of consonants in choral singing will be discussed later in this chapter.

The perception of the voice as an instrument is more than a physical image. It is a useful way of depersonalizing singing, which is subject to inhibitions and defensiveness. The average adult, however confident and mature in other respects, recoils at the idea of singing alone. Treating the voice as an instrument is objective and less threatening to the child. Thinking of the voice as an instrument tends to focus on its musical function: a means of artistic expression. The distinction between the speaking voice and the singing voice may become clearer by this analogy.

Vocal Ranges

Vocal ranges typical of various ages were described in Chapter 3 and need not be repeated here. We shall consider the relationship of range to tone quality and the cautions to be taken at both extremes of the range.

The most characteristic tone quality in children's voices is to be found in the upper register; it is certainly the most beautiful when properly produced. A large resonating space is required for higher tones. This is best created by relaxing the jaw and allowing the larynx to remain in a low, relaxed position; the director should watch for signs of strain or tension.

Most American children speak at a pitch of middle c or d, encompassing a few tones above and below. Unfortunately, they often sing with this same low voice, which results in a harsh, dead tone. Low notes (for most young singers d' and below) should be sung lightly. The most appropriate melodies in this regard will approach low notes from a fairly wide skip and will not linger in this register.

The director will be attentive to the tessitura (prevailing register) of a song and not hesitate to transpose it to a key that brings the tessitura to within the ideal range of the singers. Sometimes choristers (and their directors) are frightened by high notes, but if they are on open vowels and the general tessitura is acceptable, there is no need to lower the key. There is no danger of straining voices if the jaw is low and relaxed and the children are taught to sing lightly.

Posture

As it is breath that activates the singing mechanism, proper breathing habits are fundamental to beautiful tone and expressive phrasing. Likewise, controlled breathing begins with correct posture.

> The body is the singing voice, and like all instruments, it must be positioned precisely to function properly. The physical position of the body influences attitude as well as breathing ability and tone quality. A good singing posture not only feels, good, it looks good.[2]

Guidelines for Singing Posture

While standing:

1. Stand as if there is a string attached from the top of the head to the ceiling. Pull an imaginary string to illustrate. Show a marionette collapse, then pull up to singing posture. Pretend to be a marionette.
2. Let arms hang relaxed at sides unless holding music. Music should be held at the point where the child can see the conductor easily over the folder without lifting the head.
3. Place feet about six inches apart, one foot slightly in front.
4. Weight is primarily on the balls of the feet. Do not lock knees. Have the children bounce in place a few times to eliminate tightness.

---

[2]Doreen Rao, *The Young Singing Voice* (Boosey and Hawkes, 1987), 15.

5. Lift the chest slightly and keep the spine straight. Again, rigidity is to be avoided. Have the children reach up, as if to pick apples off a tree, then slowly lower arms and drop shoulders while keeping the rib cage high.

6. Hold the head perpendicular to the shoulders. The conductor should take care to stand where the singers can maintain this position.

While sitting:

1. Hold the upper part of the body erect, with the chest held high, as in standing.

2. Place feet flat on the floor. Do not cross the legs at the knees or ankles.

3. Lean forward slightly on the chair. Slouching interferes with the air flow and adversely affects the tone.

An important but frequently neglected factor is the type of chair used for rehearsing. The height of the chair should fit the average size of the children using them, and its design should encourage correct posture.

Young children who sit on the floor should not be permitted to lounge. Maintaining good posture is difficult in this case, so there should be frequent opportunities to stand and to move around. Children who sit in chairs should likewise change positions frequently and be allowed to sit back and relax in between periods of singing. The director may make frequent, quick posture checks during rehearsal and should always present a good example. A vitalized, buoyant posture contributes not only to proper breathing, tone production, and intonation but also to a general physical and mental alertness without which a choir will sound and look lifeless.

Breathing

Most children will not have thought much about the act of breathing, except in situations, such as swimming, where it must be conscious and controlled. It is helpful to compare singing to athletic activities in this respect, to emphasize the total physical involvement and the necessity to use the body productively. Linda Swears describes the breathing used by singers:

> Breathing for singing is deep breathing. This involves the sensation of taking air into the lowest part of the lungs first. As this occurs, the area around the lower rib cage should expand while the chest is held high and the shoulders remain stationary. As the air is expelled from the lungs it passes through the windpipe and causes the vocal cords to vibrate. This vibration produces the singing tone.[3]

---

[3]Linda Swears, *Teaching the Elementary School Chorus* (West Nyack, NY: Parker Publishing, 1985), 70.

Again, the analogy to sports is a useful one. Training the body for singing is akin to training the body for athletic events. Vocal health and stamina depend upon using the body's resources to best advantage.

The two aspects of breathing of concern to the singer are breath support and breath control. Breath support holds up the tone and helps prevent tension in the upper chest and shoulders. One does not necessarily require a large amount of breath to sing but does need a good deal of breath support.

Good breathing depends upon the correct action of the diaphragm. The diaphragm is a dome-shaped muscle located under the lungs that may be felt by placing the fingers at the bottom of the breastbone and giving a sharp puff. Deep breathing means to expand the entire midsection—in the back and around the sides as well as in front. Shallow breathing is suspected when a child lifts the shoulders while inhaling.

The breath must also be controlled as it is exhaled, in order to sustain phrases and to vary the intensity of the tone. Breathy, lifeless tone quality can usually be attributed to poor breathing habits. Here are a few suggestions for developing proper breath support and control in young singers:

1. Locate the diaphragm and pant like a dog to feel it moving. Sharp puffs or unvoiced consonants (such as *s* or *p* in a rhythm (♫ ♫ ♩𝄾)) or sung ("*ha ha ha ha ha*") on single pitch will also demonstrate the action of this muscle. Sing it on a triad, *do-mi-sol-mi-do.*

Or,

Example 6.1

Ho - ho - ho - ho - ho - ho - ho - ho -   san ___   na.   Ho - ho - ho - ho - ho

2. Count slowly on a given pitch, or chant the alphabet or some familiar rhyme or song. See who can control the breath the longest. Helen Kemp uses the image of breathing through a straw. Give the singers a "destination": sing a pitch until a signal is given (finger snap).

3. Combine staccato with sustained (inhale on the rest):

Example 6.2

ch ch ch ch ch

s   s   s   s   s   s

4. Inhale on four beats, exhale slowly on "ss" (like a locomotive). Sit down when out of air. Try the same exercise, inhaling on two counts, then only on one.

After the choristers learn how to breathe correctly for singing, they must continue to work until breath control becomes automatic. This doesn't happen overnight. Gentle reminders, visual images, and a good model (the director) continue to help. There should always be a breath cue by the director before singing begins. A rhyme that is spoken before singing will help prepare the singers. Try it in canon, too.

Example 6.3

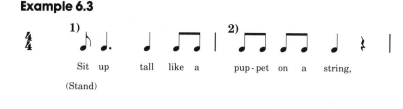

Sit up　tall like a　pup-pet on a　string,
(Stand)

Head up,　shoul-ders down,　take a breath and　sing!

Producing the Sound

The tone quality of a good children's choir is unsurpassed in beauty. To achieve this kind of sound, the director must first have a concept of the ideal tone quality toward which to strive. Roberta Bitgood asserts that "somewhere between a lifeless, thin, apathetic tone and the ugly, throaty tone that is all too common is that kind of tone which a conscientious director wants."[4] Given the variety of children who constitute the average church choir, running the gamut from poor to excellent in singing ability, there must be some uniformity of sound to achieve an acceptable choral blend. Helen Kemp cites six attributes of acceptable vocal sound:

1. The tones are clear and free, without harsh nasality or muffled throatiness.
2. Head tones are well developed but not forced.
3. Pitch is secure.
4. Full and free upper tones pass into the lower pitch range with brightness and lightness, and voices do not change gears abruptly or push out on lower tones with an obvious break.

---

[4] In *The Children's Choir*, Nancy Poore Tufts, ed. (Philadelphia: Fortress Press, 1965), 97.

5. Voices have carrying power (projection) because vowels are pure and well-focused (centered).

6. Voices keep both "ring" and "roundness" in the singing volume spectrum from p to f.[5]

One of the factors that adversely affect tone quality in children's singing is a lack of appropriate models. Too often we hear children (in professionally produced musicals or in television commercials) apparently trying to imitate the heavy, mature voices of adults; amateur choirs without proper training sing with a lackluster, breathy sound that is often excused on the basis of their personal charm. Both of these situations can be avoided. Children cannot reproduce the color and volume of an adult, and trying to do so results in a strident, unnatural tone and eventual vocal injury. The choral director must present the best possible model. It is also helpful for the children to hear live performances or recordings of good children's choirs (see Appendix C). Other factors that affect tone quality include

1. Improper breathing

2. Distorted vowels—should be uniformly shaped by the choir

3. Poor posture

4. Tension—watch for signs of strain in the neck or face.

Children are capable of producing a uniquely clear, pure, and resonant tone that seems to float. It will be lacking in vibrato and fairly colorless. Young children will not be able to sing with great dynamic contrast, and boys' and girls' voices will sound alike. The goal is a light, forward sound full of energy, vitality, and personality:

> If people say they can't hear the children, suggest they listen harder . . . It is not necessary for children to always sing softly, but it is important that they use the head placement and open throats. Loud for children need not be very loud.[6]

There are a number of techniques for achieving beautiful tone quality in young voices:

1. Emphasize correct posture and breathing.

2. Helen Kemp suggests contrasting the singing voice with the shout, the whisper, and the speaking voice. The Choristers Guild offers posters that illustrate this concept. Have the children demonstrate each and practice going from one to another.

---

[5]In *Children Sing His Praise,* Donald Rotermund, ed. (St. Louis: Concordia, 1985), 67–68.

[6]Tom Hite, "Some Ideas on Tone Building for Children's Choirs," *Journal of Church Music,* October 1987, 7.

Figure 6.2. Using a puppet to encourage open mouth, relaxed jaw.

3. Use visual or mental imagery to develop vitality in tone (stretch a rubber band vertically to represent the open, relaxed jaw; describe a leaf floating on the water to obtain buoyancy). Kemp is well known for her effective use of such visual aids, as is evident in the videocassettes listed in Appendix B.

4. Be an alert, energetic conductor. Smile. Move around and keep the singers interested.

5. Emphasize projecting the tone rather than increasing the dynamics. Having the children sing to some specific spot in the room (like an arrow or a ball going across the room). Standing farther away from the children encourages projection. Some directors place a mark on the opposite wall as a target. Sing a phrase looking down, then at the target for contrast.

6. Work on vowel formation, shaping each uniformly. Vowels carry the tone and affect choral blend and intonation as well. Practice sustaining the pure vowels (*ah, ay, ee, oh, oo*) without distortion and lis-

ten to the unique color of each. Vocalize downward, to carry the head voice into the middle register.

Example 6.4

Al - le - lu - ia,   Al - le - lu - ia.
Al - le - lu - ia,   Al - le - lu - ia.   Al - le -

7. Occasionally practice a piece of music on *loo* or just the vowel sounds to focus on the tone quality.

8. Develop activities to emphasize a chosen vowel sound.

> $\frac{6}{8}$ Oodles of noodles, oodles of noodles,
> I could eat oodles and oodles of noodles,
> Because I love noodles the best of all foodles,
> (snap)   ♩.   ♩.   Truly I do!

Activities:

a. Speak the poem rhythmically in $\frac{6}{8}$ meter.

b. Speak only the *oo* sounds, "thinking" the rest.

c. Sing the rhyme on one note.

d. Sing it on two- or three-note chords.

9. Contrast two vowel sounds.

Example 6.5

Loo bee loo bee loo bee loo bee   loo bee loo bee loo.   Loo bee loo bee . . .

10. Vocalize on *noo* or *zee* for a bright, forward, resonant tone.

11. Emphasize the relaxed open jaw and throat, free of tension. Stop and yawn. Vocalize on *nah* or *yah*.

12. Do not sing with the children routinely. Rather, *listen*. Train the singers to listen to themselves, tape (audio or video) their singing for playback, or occasionally divide the choir.

The director must translate his or her concept of tone quality into verbal and visual imagery that is understood by the children. When that sound is achieved, the choir should be helped to recognize it so that it can be reproduced. Habitual beauty of tone requires constant effort, but it becomes its own reward.

Intonation

Henry Higgins in *My Fair Lady* bemoans the painful effects of a choir singing flat, an experience all too familiar to most of us. Good intonation is the result of proper posture and tone production, careful listening, and certain environmental factors. All choirs must cultivate an awareness of pitch, especially as it relates to the total ensemble sound. For most choirs, the pitch tends to be flat rather than sharp. Even when the children are able to match pitch and sing in tune with each other, the choir may nevertheless experience intonation difficulties.

Some possible causes, and remedies, for flatting are the following:

1. The room is too warm. Open the windows or otherwise relieve the stuffy atmosphere.

2. The children are tired. Is it late in the day? Have the singers been sitting or standing too long? Try some moderately paced warm-ups involving movement.

3. The music is in an inappropriate key. Is it generally too high? Perhaps it is too low—try putting it up a half step. Sometimes it is a matter of finding a brighter key.

4. The children are using poor posture and breathing habits.

5. The children are insecure with the music.

6. The singing is forced and too loud. Ask for light head voice and careful listening. Forcing can also cause the singing to go sharp. Making the children aware of the problem is part of the solution. "Think" the pitch before singing.

7. The children may not understand what it means to sing flat. Use imagery to convey the idea—a bird lighting on top of the branch, not hanging from it. Sing "through the eyes," in Helen Kemp's language. Demonstrate flat singing and contrast it with correct intonation.

8. The accompaniment interferes. Is it too loud or too heavy? Have the singers come to rely on it too much? Do more a cappella rehearsing.

9. The vocal line descends; singers often drop a little too much on each descending pitch. Point up slightly as the phrase descends as a reminder to "think high." Repeated notes often invite sagging pitch, too.

10. There is a generalized apathy and sluggishness. Perhaps the singers do not like the music. The director in this case needs to demonstrate a vitality and a sparkle that may energize the group. Changing the pace or the activity itself may restore some of the alertness.

11. The singing may be lacking in that rhythmic drive which propels the melody line. Stop and work on the rhythm itself—speaking it or clapping it—keeping a steady pulse and a flowing rhythm. The psychological effects of this rejuvenation may carry over into pitch. Or temporarily try a slower tempo and take time to listen to individual pitches.

12. Dark vowels give the effect of lowering pitches. Brighten vowels to "sharpen" the pitch.

Diction

Unless good diction is practiced, choirs are singing "songs without words." Sloppy speech patterns are common, and children learn them from people around them. Group singing naturally distorts speech anyway by sustaining syllables, adding substantial pitch and dynamic variety, and combining vocal colors. In the case of part-singing and polyphonic textures, words may not even be sung simultaneously. Consequently, good diction is paramount if the text is to be understood.

While pronunciation gives meaning and is one aspect of diction, enunciation of vowels and articulation of consonants are more troublesome to the singers unless the text is in a language foreign to them. Vowels shape and sustain the tone. In addition to the pure *ah ay ee oh oo,* they may be long or short in sound. Choir children will be familiar with these from their study of phonetics in school.

Uniformity of vowel sounds contributes to tone quality and overall blend of the group. Vocalizing on the pure vowels (above) is helpful if the children transfer this to music being learned. Preceding the vowels with the consonant *n* brings the vowel forward. Sing on one pitch,

Example 6.6

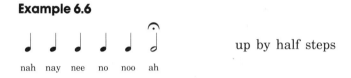

nah   nay   nee   no   noo   ah   up by half steps

Closed vowels (*ee* and *oo*) are so called because they are formed with the jaw elevated and the mouth slightly closed. All other vowels are referred to as open vowels, with the jaw being lowest and most relaxed on the vowel *ah.* Vowels are often modified to accommodate the singer at different registers, to alter the color of the text, or to improve intonation.

Singing a phrase with consonants and then with only the vowels may help unify those sounds.

Example 6.7

See if the children can identify a familiar rhyme or song by the vowels alone:

> *ee uh   uh   ee   ih   ah-ee oh*
> (Je-sus loves me, this I know)

When two vowels are combined, they are known as diphthongs. In singing, one or the other is stressed (sustained). For example:

> light = *AH* + *ee*   loud = *AH* + *oo*   new = *ee* + *OO*

Consonants

Consonants are not sustained and are used to make the text understandable. Every consonant must thus be audible, but many singers are careless with this aspect of diction.

Some consonants have pitch: *b, d, j, g (go), m, n, ng, l, v, z, w, y,* and *th (the)*. Unvoiced consonants are *p, th (thin), h, t, k, s, sh,* and *f*. Consonants that may be hummed (*m, n,* and *ng*) are useful in vocalizing for resonance or head tone (see above). Vibrations felt during humming are easily identified by the choristers.

Singers must sustain vowel sounds as long as possible, not moving to the consonant too quickly. This is to keep the vocal mechanism open and the tone undistorted.

One frequent speech disorder is the omission of certain sounds, final consonants being the most commonly omitted. All consonants, particularly beginning and final ones, must be rhythmically precise in a choral ensemble.

Practice rhymes, spoken or sung,

Example 6.8

Here comes the la - dy with the   big   green   hat.

The final *t* occurs on the rest.

Unvoiced consonants may be practiced in a speech warm-up. (Use phonetic sounds.)

Example 6.9

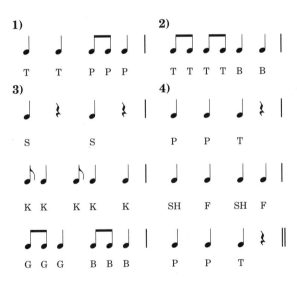

Some consonants are occasionally omitted altogether in singing. The final *r* is troublesome as it blocks and thus distorts the tone. Some directors recommend omitting or just "thinking" the *r* when it occurs at the end of a word or just before another consonant *(Lord)*. The consonant *s* is also a potential problem unless it is articulated very quickly and rhythmically, as it can produce a prolonged hiss or, in a choir, a series of hisses. Ehmann and Hassemann suggest many practical vocalises for consonants and vowels alike.[7]

---

[7]Wilhelm Ehmann and Frauke Hassemann, *Voice Building for Choirs* (Chapel Hill, NC: Hinshaw Music, 1982).

Tongue twisters make interesting articulators (to exercise the tongue and lips) and focus on specific consonant sounds. Say a selected word over and over, rhythmically and with increasing speed: *linoleum; sweet potato; purple pelican.*

Example 6.10

(1) Car-rie car-ried Car-men off to Can - a - da.   Car-rie car-ried

(2) A   big black bug bit a   big black bear and the   big black bear bled   bad-ly.

A   big black bug bit a   big black bear and the   big black bear bled   bad - ly.

A   big black bug bit a   big black bear and the   big black bear bled   bad - ly.

Vocal flexibility may be developed through short exercises at a fast tempo.

Example 6.11

(1) La la la la la   la   la la la la la   la la la la la la la la   la   la   la

La — la — la   la ____   La _____   la   la

Co - co-nut co - co-nut   co - co-nut co - co-nut   co - co-nut co - co-nut   co - co-nut pie.

Co - co-nut co - co-nut   co - co-nut co - co-nut   co - co-nut co - co-nut   co - co-nut pie.

–Tammy Grant, used with permission

Vocalises of any kind are most helpful when directly related to problems in the music being learned or created for specific vocal situations. The exercises themselves should be practiced in a musical manner and scattered throughout the rehearsal as needed. Five minutes of vocalizing at the beginning of the rehearsal tends to become routine and unrelated to real musical situations.

SINGING IN TUNE

Singing in tune means reproducing (matching) the pitches presented by an instrument or another singer. Much has made of this skill throughout the recent history of music education, sometimes to the humiliation of the child who cannot do it. Fortunately, most normal children acquire this ability without conscious effort, but for others individual assistance is needed.

Singing in tune consists of three processes: perceiving the sound, remembering the sound and producing it vocally, and recognizing whether or not they are the same. In other words, there is an auditory component (receiving and retaining the sound) and a kinesthetic one (manipulating the voice appropriately and coordinating it with the ear).

Out-of-tune singing manifests itself in two ways: the drone, singing in a very limited range and in a low register; and singing recognizable melodies but at a different pitch (usually lower) from other singers. The so-called "monotone" is generally considered very rare.

A child who is physically and mentally normal can, under the right circumstances, be taught to sing in tune. Progress is dependent upon individual help, an accepting environment, and a competent teacher:

> It is absolutely imperative that the teacher in such a situation make mistakes an acceptable part of learning. The child who cannot sing in tune must be made to feel by every action, word, and look that the class and the teacher

accept that child as a person, while work continues on the skill. With the example of the teacher before them, young children can be very supportive of each other. Acceptance or rejection must not be fastened to skill performance, or children will be afraid to try anything.[8]

Choksy goes on to point out that "acceptance" by no means implies pretending that every response is "fine." Nothing destroys a trusting relationship faster than this kind of dishonesty, since the children soon recognize it for what it is. A constructive environment requires a frank but objective appraisal and a supportive approach in dealing with the situation. Helping the child in a matter-of-fact way to understand just what the problem is, combined with honest praise ("That was better that time, John. You are making progress!") *when deserved,* improves both the skill and the attitude. Our voices are intimately tied to our self-esteem, and we want to use music experiences that increase, not reduce, the child's sense of personal worth.

Pitch Problems

1. The child is lacking in musical experience. For whatever reasons, many children reach school age ignorant of nursery rhymes and lacking experiences in vocal and rhythmic play. The importance of very early exposure to music cannot be discounted. Thus, the child who has never sung or been sung *to* or encouraged to play with sounds and rhythms, comes to the choir at a disadvantage. Fortunately, regular participation in happy musical activities will sometimes bring results rather quickly.

2. The child is very timid and self-conscious. Singing may be almost inaudible. Care should be taken that music experiences do not bring about tension.

3. The child has not distinguished between the singing and speaking voice. This is one of the more common causes of out-of-tune singing but perhaps the easiest to remedy, since vocal play with the entire group is possible. Children who attempt to sing in their speaking voice may be emulating the style of some popular singers. They may also have been exhorted to "sing louder" or have sung in keys too low for them.

4. The child is basically immature, physically and socially. Sometimes, given even casual experience with music, patience, and time to grow, this child may suddenly catch up vocally with his or her peers.

5. The child has poor posture and breathing habits. This condition is hardly conducive to good singing by anyone, especially the child who is unable physically to control the singing voice.

---

[8]Lois Choksy, *The Kodály Context* (Englewood Cliffs, NJ: Prentice-Hall, 1981), 81.

6. The tempo is too fast. The young child's faster body tempo does not apply here. There needs to be time to hear and absorb the tones that are to be reproduced. The teacher should give plenty of time to hear the first pitch before beginning and then maintain a relaxed tempo for the duration of the song.

7. The intervals are too difficult. Early pitch-matching is usually more successful if melodies are confined to *sol-la-mi* and extended to include *do-re*.

8. The child is singing too loud. This situation inhibits the hearing process as well as contributing to undesirable tone quality.

Remedies

In addition to the remedies implied in the above list of causes, there are a number of techniques that may be used with the choir as a whole or with the individual.

1. Make individual singing a routine affair. Circle games, in which each child participates briefly, are fun and give the director a chance to hear individual voices.

Example 6.12

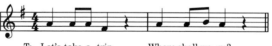

T: Let's take a trip.   Where shall we go?

C: Let's go   to   A - las - ka!

Young children are not usually inhibited by solo singing until they somehow get the message that they are being judged. A gamelike atmosphere will minimize that possibility.

   (a) Pass a bag of small objects, from which the child will draw one and sing about it. ("I found a crayon.")

   (b) Give each child a card with a picture of an animal (or foods or toys) on it. The child responds "I have the apple" when the director sings "Who has the apple?"

2. Use dramatization songs and props. Finger plays, action songs, and puppets take attention away from the singer. The child as-

sumes another identity through the puppet and tends to relax. The puppet (teacher's voice) may sing to the child, or the child may have a puppet as well.

3. Make regular opportunities to contrast the singing and speaking voice. Say a phrase to the choir, then sing it. Or tell a story, switching from speech to song, and have the children identify each as it occurs. Have the children echo speech patterns expressively, then simple melodies using the same text. Let individual children speak or sing a line of a poem or a phrase from Scripture, and the group imitate. Encourage changes in pitch, dynamics, or tempo. This exercise may also be done with partners. A simple drawing can be held up to remind the singers to use the light singing voice.

Figure 6.3. Not too loud!

The director should use very expressive speech at all times as well as modeling the proper singing voice. Opportunities to echo spoken phrases, not matching exact pitches but demonstrating light and heavy voices, are helpful.

4. The droning child needs the kinesthetic sensation of using the higher range properly. Extremes of range are called for, so that the child feels how the voice moves—such as imitating a siren, wind, ghosts, or a fire engine in a glissando pattern. Move a toy car up

and down a hill (drawn on the board or simply in the air) for voices to follow. The *oo* vowel has been found to be easiest for the child to hear and feel.

5. Vocal flexibility may be helped by asking the voice to "follow" the arc of a beanbag as it is tossed, or a scarf or a feather.

6. Improvise an "opera." Given a brief scenario, the children sing (individually) the narration and dialogue. The material may be a known fable or fairy tale or some everyday event, like getting ready for school in the morning. Melodrama is encouraged, and everything is impromptu, freeing the children from fear of doing something wrong.

7. Melodies of limited range are more realistic than are those encompassing an octave or more.

8. Play numerous high-low identification games, emphasizing extremes at first, then narrowing the range. Play a pitch on the piano and then play or sing another one, asking it if is higher or lower. The children may, with eyes closed, raise their hands on high pitches played on the piano and lower them for low pitches.

9. Give opportunities to identify unison pitches. Play a note on the piano or ask a child to sing a pitch, then match it or sing a different one. Ask the child (or choir) if the pitch is the same or different. Some directors find it successful to match a droning child's pitch and then raise it gradually. Choksy in *The Kodály Context* disputes this, maintaining that it is impossible to raise the chest voice in such a way. At any rate, the child needs to be able to recognize what is unison and what is not.

10. Try visual and kinesthetic aids. Pitch is an abstract idea, and high-low is often confused with loud-soft. The child, thinking in concrete terms, relates to ladders, elevators, hands moving up and down, and other visual representations of vertical direction. The hand signals associated with the Kodály approach illustrated on page 68 are valuable in that the child supports kinesthetically the pitch direction of a melody.

11. Seat the uncertain singer between two strong singers. This is an indirect way of confronting the problem, but it may help.

12. Ask the children to cup their hands behind their ears while singing. This simple technique aids the listening process.

13. Encourage parental involvement. Most parents can use simple tone-matching techniques with their child, or if there is reluctance, a prepared audiocassette could be sent home. Additional music experiences—listening to recordings, playing simple instruments, singing to the child—will complement specific remediation by the choir director.

14. If the child has difficulty matching a pitch from the piano or voice, try a tenor recorder, melody bells, or alto metallophone.
15. Try to help all children realize that, just as in sports or any subject in school, singing comes easier for some people. Needing extra help is not a disgrace and therefore can usually be dealt with in an open and matter-of-fact manner within the rehearsal. Let the choir be the support system for the uncertain singers, sharing in the pleasure of every indication of progress.

Sometimes an entire choir can sound out-of-tune. In this case there are several considerations.

1. Do the children have an overall perception of the song? Sing several phrases for them. Ask them to close their eyes as they listen.

2. Make sure they hear the starting pitch clearly before they begin to sing. Ask small groups to match the beginning pitch on *loo*. Try the opening melodic motive—sometimes this is easier to reproduce than a single isolated pitch.

3. Is there interference in the environment? Some children cannot "tune out" competing sounds around them. Try to minimize any aural or other distractions.

4. If accompaniment is used, it is appropriate?

- If piano, it should be soft but clear, with a transparent texture free of thick, heavy chords and excessive ornamentation.
- If organ, light diapason or reed stops and light pedal are recommended. Flute stops, which are similar to the timbre of the children's voices, and vibrato are usually ineffective.
- Orff instruments should provide contrast in color and range. Glockenspiels are useful to add brilliance. Children sometimes have difficulty at first finding their pitch from an introduction played on bass instruments alone.

THE CHANGING VOICE

While the scope of this book is confined to treble (unchanged) voices, the director and the choir need to be aware of the physiological changes that will occur. Children mature at varying rates, and it is no longer unusual for such changes to begin in late elementary years.

The most important consideration is that the children recognize the change as a natural occurrence as boys and girls grow up, although it is much more dramatic in boys. Most experts agree that boys should continue to sing during the transition if healthy vocal habits are maintained:

The boys in vocal transition should be carefully monitored as maturation progresses. They should be encouraged to breathe more frequently and to maintain an appropriate singing posture at all times. As the range changes from treble to bass clef, it is important to vocalize the boys from where they sing most comfortably (which is often high in treble II range, down through the middle register) where they will have to "lighten" and support carefully through the "new territory" of the baritone range. It is crucial not to limit the changing voice to the "falsetto" sound, but to encourage a vital and healthy connection to the head voice as it is exercised throughout the *entire* range.[9]

The director needs to watch for signs of change. The most obvious changes occur in stature and physique. Other evidence is found in the speaking voice, which may take on a husky quality before any actual lowering of pitch. At some point there will be loss of the top notes of the voice and an extension of the lower range. During this transition period, the director should listen to the child's voice from time to time and take care that it is not placed under any strain in the choral experience. Use of the head voice should be continued, as well as good habits of posture and breathing. Above all, positive attitudes about singing and music will help offset any awkwardness or self-consciousness.

SUMMARY

Good singing habits begin in elementary choral experiences and help ensure future vocal health. Besides presenting a good example, the ensemble director can help children understand the vocal mechanism and how to use it expressively in speech and song. Proper posture and breathing should be fostered in young singers in order to produce the uniquely beautiful sounds of which they are capable. Good intonation and diction may be taught through simple vocalises but should be cultivated in every musical context. The church choral experience, to be consistent with the ideals we have set forth, should satisfy both the spiritual and artistic needs of the child.

---

[9]Doreen Rao, *The Young Singing Voice,* 22.

CHAPTER 7

The Rehearsal

"If we taught children to speak, they would never learn."
—WILLIAM HULL

The above quotation would seem to declare the futility of the teaching process, at least in the conventional sense. Most of us have assumed that teaching is always a conscious act, carried on by certain individuals, usually adults, who themselves have been "trained" to teach. Moreover, this process occurs in a place and time designated, or set aside, for teaching and learning to take place. A final assumption, and an erroneous one, is that "learning" necessarily follows "teaching." Many of us have heard or made the statement, "Well, I just don't know why that child didn't learn it—I certainly *taught* it!"

The children's choir director may be susceptible to a kind of panic when confronted with the multiplicity of things to be accomplished within a single rehearsal. How is it possible—there's the music to be learned for Sunday, plus the festival coming up in a few weeks, and musicianship skills can't be neglected. And Susie requested her favorite fun song this week. Besides, there were several children absent last week, and we've got to review some things for them. Something's got to give.

What needs to happen is threefold: an awareness of how children learn, careful planning, and flexibility within the rehearsal. Children respond differently at each stage of their development, but they generally remember what they deem to be important at the time. If adults set out to teach them to speak, no doubt we would organize and structure the task in such a way that children would be baffled and discouraged, and some of them would even fail. But we *taught* them! *Teaching* music is likely to be the same way. We think the child must acquire specific skills with the expectation that they will someday make music interesting and useful for that child. It makes more sense, at least to the child, to start with enjoyable music experiences and provide the skills necessary for them. Most other kinds of motivation are artificial and are recognized as such by the child.

Back to the original problem, then: what is important in a rehearsal? How can we accomplish what we have set out to do? Most of what contributes to a successful rehearsal happens well in advance of the rehearsal itself. Given the constraints of time (usually an hour at best) and attendance (which is voluntary), the director must rely on careful planning and organization to make the most of the precious rehearsal time. This chapter will consider the principles of a successful rehearsal, the first of them being planning.

PRINCIPLES OF A SUCCESSFUL REHEARSAL

Planning

Know the music. This means sitting down with each score and analyzing it, picking out the musical characteristics.

1. What is the overall form of the piece? Are there repeated sections? If some phrases or sections are similar but not identical, how are they different? What difficulty will this pose in teaching it to the singers?

2. What about the rhythmic characteristics? Is the piece full of syncopations or some particular rhythmic figure? Is the rhythm natural—compatible with the rhythm of the text? How do the meter and rhythm affect the character of the piece?

3. What is the melody like? Is it basically diatonic? pentatonic? stepwise? full of skips? Are there repeated motives or phrases? Is it supported by the harmonic structure?

4. What are the expressive elements of the piece? Note dynamic and tempo changes and any departure from smooth legato singing.

5. For what instruments is the accompaniment scored, and how does it contribute to the overall character of the piece? Is it independent of the vocal line, or does it simply support it?

Next, take a look at the words of the anthem or song. What are the theological concepts contained in the text? Is its message generally comprehensible to the children or could it be understood given some brief and simple discussion? Are the ideas compatible with those of the congregation and are they worth knowing in the first place? There are many noble and poetic texts available in children's repertoire, and resorting to childish, mediocre ones that will soon be discarded is indefensible.

Besides theological concepts, there are musical concepts within any piece of music that may be taught. Matters of form, texture, melody, rhythm, and harmony will become apparent to the director in analyzing the piece. Some of these, as well as pertinent expressive elements, may be pointed out to the choristers during rehearsal or used as the basis for an activity to develop musicianship skills.

As the director studies the piece, certain enrichment activities might well come to mind—activities to deepen the understanding of the text or the music. For example, there might be a study of the author or the composer. There might be related Scripture, poetry, or artwork to enhance the meaning of the piece. Games and puzzles to aid in the learning of the piece are fun and are convenient as take-home reminders of what the choir is singing. Some choirs like to add interpretive movement to their music, and perhaps a few children, if not all, could share in this unique method of expressing words and melody.

Most experienced directors of singers of any age have accumulated a repertoire of favorite warm-ups and vocalises for a variety of situations. They are able to pull them out on the spot, as the need arises within a piece of music or as vocal problems surface. Nevertheless, most directors would be wise to anticipate what exercises might be appropriate for the vocal and musical requirements of the piece at hand. As was pointed out in Chapter 6, technical warm-ups are most effective when directly related to a given task or situation.

Perhaps the musical arrangement needs a few modifications in order to be usable. If there is to be a key change, for example, the accompanist needs time to prepare for this. Sometimes instrument parts need to be deleted or supplemented, and occasionally the director will want to create some. Any other accompaniment changes are best noted in the early stages, as well as alterations in the vocal score itself—such as deletion of second or third parts, or entire sections. Major overhauling of a piece of music is of course not fair to the composer—or to the piece, for that matter—and should be avoided, but minor alterations to accommodate individual needs should be acceptable. Care must always be taken to respect the integrity and general character of the music.

Almost any piece has within it some potential problem spots for the musicians. The director who can spot these problems before they actually occur is in a position to solve them more easily, if not prevent them altogether. Close examination of the music, along with a knowledge of how children sing, can help the director predict what those problems may be and prepare strategies for dealing with them. For example, there may be difficult intervals that will surely cause trouble. The text may reveal potential diction problems. There may be difficult entrances, long phrases, rhythmic complexities, meter changes, conflict with the accompaniment, and the like. Making sure that the children learn things correctly in the beginning pays off in terms of time saved and frustration avoided.

The director, in studying the score, may think of imaginative ways to introduce the new music. Perhaps there are characteristic rhythms or melodic motives that may be used in warm-ups to introduce the piece. Or maybe something said about the composer or author can inspire interest in starting a new piece. Almost every piece has something distinctive about it that could be used to introduce it. Always approaching a new anthem in the same way becomes predictable and boring.

Finally, knowing the music means just that: being thoroughly familiar with it so that attention can be given to the singers themselves. If the director is tentative about a piece and keeps eyes constantly on the score, that uncertainty will transfer to the children. Furthermore, they cannot be expected to watch the director if that director's eyes are always somewhere else.

Prepare visual aids. Most teaching is more effective if there are attractive visual aids to capture attention. These do not need to be elaborate, but to serve the purpose they must be large enough to be seen or read by all the children. The chalkboard is indispensable, but prepared diagrams, drawings, and objects are effective and worth having ready. Written reminders posted in a conspicuous place eliminate the need for so much "teacher talk." Melodic motives or ostinato patterns to be played may be written on large staff paper, laminated if desired, and placed in view before rehearsal begins. Such preparation prevents pacing lags in the rehearsal while the director writes something on the board. At any rate, this appeal to the visual sense can reinforce the listening skills required for music activities.

Communication

The children's choir director is in the business of communication, as is any educator. Communication in this context means interacting with the children, verbally and nonverbally, in an environment that fosters experimentation, discovery, and musical and spiritual growth. In other words, the teacher/director must first of all make sure that everyone is comfortable and at ease, and then use words, gestures, and facial expressions that make sense to the children. Being comfortable in the environment depends in part upon the room itself and the arrangement of the chairs. Formal arrangements, with chairs in straight rows, tend to separate those in the back from the mainstream of the group and inhibit participation. Very young children, and sometimes older ones, often do well sitting on the floor, in which case the director should sit on the floor with them. The casual friendliness of such an arrangement, plus the fact that in a circle everyone is equal, communicates acceptance. See the diagrams for room arrangements in Chapter 5 for specific suggestions. An important aspect of communication, often overlooked, is listening to and watching the responses of the singers. Communication is much more than sending one-way messages; it is also receiving messages and responding to them. Choral directors sometimes fall victim to the practice of routinely singing along with their ensemble, thus failing to listen to what is being sung. At best it distorts the sound. In general, communication may be verbal or nonverbal, most often combining elements of each.

Verbal Communication

1. The first suggestion regarding words is not to use too many of them! Most teachers would be more effective if they talked less and listened more. Tape a rehearsal to see how much unnecessary talking went on.

2. Since it is annoying for everyone when instructions must be repeated, get the group's attention first and then say what is to be said only once. If the children listen but do not understand, say it in a different way. Make this practice a habit.

3. When verbal instructions are used, make sure they are simple and direct. Children "tune out" lengthy directions, which tend to be redundant anyway.

4. Speak in a well-modulated voice. If the group is noisy, do not speak louder but wait until they are quiet. Vary the dynamic level; occasional whispering can be very effective.

5. Speak in language that the children can understand. This does not mean resorting to slang or cute language and certainly not in a patronizing manner. It simply means acknowledging the child's world (interests, heroes, experiences) and relating to it.

6. Maintain a courteous, respectful manner. Displays of irritation tend to impede communication. Patience, a positive attitude, and a sense of humor are more productive. Be generous with praise, when deserved.

Nonverbal Communication

1. Replace unnecessary words with signals, posters, or other visual reminders handily placed in the room. Signals may be developed to indicate directions of many kinds: stand, sit in singing posture, relax, stop talking, and so on. Signs may remind the singers to correct their posture or use their singing voices, and the like. Half a minute of echo-clapping brings a group happily to attention—and faster than verbal directions.

2. Maintain eye contact with all the children. Some teachers tend to look at certain individuals or one side of the group most of the time. Cultivate the practice of looking directly at the children; let them know they are truly seen.

3. Move around among the children. Do not be afraid to stray away from the music stand. If they are seated on the floor, join them there.

4. Maintain a pleasant, alert expression. Smiling sends a message that the children are liked and that the rehearsal is enjoyable.

5. A nod of approval or an inconspicuous pat on the back can encourage a faltering chorister without causing embarrassing attention.

Conducting

The ultimate nonverbal form of communication with the singers is the act of conducting. Gestures, body movement, and facial expressions combine to create a system that tells the choristers when and how to perform the music. The director should be competent in the basic conducting patterns and extend them to include a variety of techniques for making an artistic rendition. Standard conducting patterns in common meters are pictured below. Non-espressivo movements are more or less crisp and well defined, while espressivo-legato movements are used to convey a flowing melodic line.

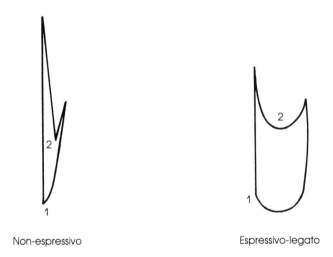

Non-espressivo   Espressivo-legato

Figure 7.1. The Two-Beat Pattern.

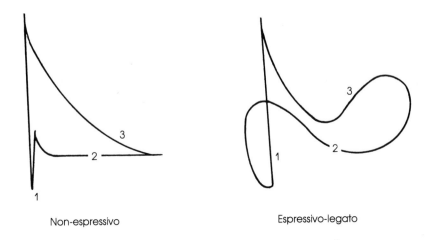

Non-espressivo   Espressivo-legato

Figure 7.2. The Three-Beat Pattern.

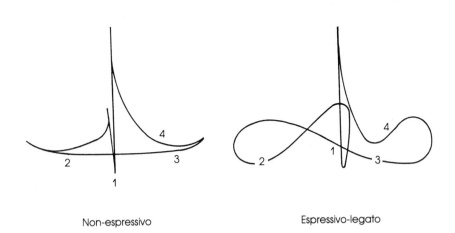

Non-espressivo   Espressivo-legato

Figure 7.3. The Four-Beat Pattern.

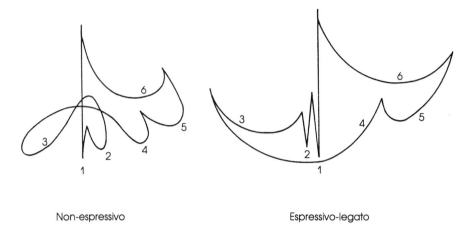

Non-espressivo   Espressivo-legato

Figure 7.4. The Six-Beat Pattern.

Meters of five or seven may be treated as combinations of two + three or three + four, respectively. Conducting patterns depend upon the natural groupings, for example, in $\frac{5}{4}$ meter, 2 + 3 or 3 + 2. Conducting gestures must be automatic with the right arm, freeing the left for cues and matters of interpretation. This process is difficult for the beginner, who is advised to practice exercises such as inscribing a circle with one hand while beating up and down with the other. It is not good practice for the left arm to mirror the right, except on occasion for emphasis or if the ensemble is very large and some singers are at a distance from the conductor.

Choral conducting is nonverbal communication and as such should make use of many subtle ways of sending messages to the singers. One of these is facial expression. Children seem to be especially responsive to this aspect of direction, reflecting themselves the vitality, sparkle, and involvement of their conductor. The importance of eye contact cannot be overemphasized. Therefore, memorizing music to be performed is well worth the effort, as children and director can maintain fairly constant eye contact. Scowling conductors who keep their eyes on the score communicate to the choristers that they are not fully present but somehow alone with the music, and furthermore that they are not enjoying the experience very much.

The conductor is essentially a reminder. The children cannot be counted on to remember all the aspects of a musical presentation, no matter how meticulous their preparation. In a performance, all messages must be sent nonverbally. Reminders of when and how to stand or sit, intonation, tempo or meter changes, and cues of all sorts must be given in time for the children to respond correctly. Some cues, such as crescendos, accelerandos, sustained holds, and the like, are given at the moment they are needed.

Rehearsal Management

Smooth rehearsals don't just happen. A variety of conditions must be present for the rehearsal to flow happily from one activity to the next, the children listening attentively, participating eagerly, and contributing actively to the development of skills and artistry in performance. Naturally there are times when things go awry in spite of the most careful preparation, just as there are occasions when everything seems to fall into place without apparent effort. The management of a successful rehearsal depends upon all the conditions in the environment that affect morale and learning. Most of us translate this as discipline, or control of the children.

In fact, discipline is indeed a matter of universal concern to directors of children's choirs. Without a manageable environment, musical growth cannot take place, and everyone's morale suffers. In a volunteer organization such as a church choir, it is especially important to maintain a positive, rewarding atmosphere free of threats, intimidation, and punishment. After all, all children are welcome—indeed, encouraged—to participate. At the same time, a chaotic environment cannot be productive, and disruptive behavior cannot be tolerated. This is for the benefit of everyone, not just the well-being of the director. Three components of rehearsal management will be considered, with specific suggestions offered within each: motivation, personality, and planning and structure.

Motivation

1. Maintain a set of rules, clearly established and uniformly enforced. A few simple rules are easier to manage than an intricate legal system. The more rules there are, the more there are to break!

2. Use positive reinforcement of good behavior. Comment on good posture, attentiveness, and the like; try to ignore minor infractions.

3. Approach discipline positively. For example, instead of reprimands about gum-chewing during rehearsal, simply collect it all at the beginning.

4. Let the problem be that of the choir, not the director: "Look, we're really wasting time right now, and I had hoped we would be able to play the instruments today."

5. Emphasize rewards. Yearly awards, festivals, and parties are nice, but remember the short-term awards. "If we can finish all our music for Sunday, we'll have time for that game you asked for." Some directors give awards in the form of simple designs on paper for being on time or finding hymns quickly.[1]

---

[1] Delores Hruby, "Signs and Wonders, Part II," *Choristers Guild Letters*, January 1987, 128.

6. In a church choir, maintain a spiritual orientation—a sense of dedication and service. Encourage teamwork and cooperation.

7. Treat the children as worthy musicians and emphasize their importance in the choir. Maintain high expectations and a belief in their ability to achieve. Involve them in evaluating their own performance.

8. Build morale by allowing individual children to be leaders in various activities.

9. Build a sense of pride in the accomplishments of the choir. Take pictures, make recordings, and publicize their activities.

Personality

1. Avoid personalizing things. The children should not be expected to behave or perform well *for the director,* nor should they be led to believe their failure to do well is a personal affront. By the same token, disapproval of a behavior should not be communicated as rejection of the child.

2. "Let bygones be bygones." Do not let a misbehaving child sense any hostility on other occasions. Continue to be friendly and accept that child as a person.

3. Speak frankly but privately to a child who continually misbehaves: "You know, I find your constant talking very annoying, and so do the other children. Besides, it takes up time we need to do other things. I want to help you remember to wait until the right time to talk."

4. Avoid sarcasm and rudeness, and do not permit it in the group.

5. Keep a sense of humor. Try to distinguish genuine disruptiveness from occasional mischief.

6. Always display a loving and caring attitude—for the children and for the shared musical experience.

7. Be consistent. Do not overlook a behavior one day and punish the same act on another.

8. Try to understand why a child is a perpetual offender.[2]

9. Cultivate an air of calm confidence.

Planning and Structure

1. Allow time for the children to talk, then insist on quiet the rest of the time. Be reasonable.

---

[2]Arthur Eichhorn offers some excellent insights in his article "Discipline in Your Children's Choir," *Choristers Guild Letters,* April 1988, 197.

2. Have a seating arrangement and stick to it until necessary to change.

3. Keep things moving along. Be sensitive to young attention spans and change the activity when there is generalized restlessness.

4. Put variety into the rehearsal. Give time to move, to relax. Alternate active with quiet, new with familiar.

5. Have more than enough activities planned for a given rehearsal. Avoid unnecessary lags. Have visual aids and a written plan ready.

6. Have a last resort in mind for an offending behavior and follow through on it if necessary. Empty threats encourage misbehavior.

7. Instead of talking all the time, use signals and signs as reminders. See Communication section above.

8. Protect the positive environment. Try to remove distracting elements in or outside the room. Prevent interruptions if possible.

9. Learn each child's name as quickly as possible. Use names liberally in rehearsal.

Agenda

The best rehearsals follow a plan. This plan should include all music that is to be rehearsed plus all other activities designed to enrich the choir experience, and these elements need to be thoughtfully arranged in an order that respects the nature of children and how they learn. Much has been said about this subject already. Let us now list some items that are likely to be present in a rehearsal, without regard to order.

1. Spiritual growth: The special purpose of a church choir should be reflected in the spirit of the rehearsal. Spoken or sung prayers and Scripture readings may reinforce this function.

2. Business items: Roll must be taken each week. There will be announcements of various kinds—events, services, rehearsals, and so on. Any birthdays to be recognized or weekly awards to be presented are included.

3. Warm-up song: Most children (and adults) make the transition into choir rehearsal better if their bodies, minds, and voices are stimulated. Other vocalizing for tone quality, diction, and flexibility needs to be included, preferably related to specific musical situations.

4. Review: Each rehearsal will probably include expansion of material begun at previous rehearsals. Often a new element is added, but repetition is important for children.

5. New material: Something new, however trivial, enlivens the routine of a rehearsal. Add the elements of surprise, mystery, and anticipation.

6. Movement: Most children, especially the younger ones, will need something active during the rehearsal. Confining them to their chairs is contrary to the nature of children.

7. Hymns: A review of hymns for the Sunday service, or regular hymn study, is very important in children's choirs. Keep a record of hymns learned in a conspicuous place and review them from time to time. Help the children learn to use the hymnal.

8. Service music: Any service music that the choir will sing in the next service should be included—responses, doxologies, and the like.

9. Special study or project: Occasional enrichment studies, games, and projects give depth and variety to the choir program. Samples of these are provided in Chapter 8.

10. Musicianship: Any games, exercises, or other activities designed to develop musicianship skills and not incorporated into other music-learning should be a regular part of the rehearsal.

11. Performance mechanics: Children need to rehearse every move for a performance in a service. They should know ahead of time where they are to sit, where they will stand to sing, and how to get there. They need to know where to get their materials and where to put them after the service. They should practice in the place where they will be singing. If the organ is to be used, practice more than once with this accompaniment.

GENERIC REHEARSAL SCHEDULE

The following outline suggests how an anthem might be prepared over five rehearsals. It does not refer to any specific material but presumes a two-part anthem, with keyboard and one or two additional melody or percussion instruments.

Before First Rehearsal

1. Give music to the accompanist and other instrumentalists two weeks in advance. If possible, go over the music with them to clarify tempi, dynamics, and other elements.

2. Write out any transpositions or modifications to the score.

3. Analyze and learn the music thoroughly. Memorize, if possible, for the most authoritative conducting.

4. Make any necessary visual aids and create vocalises.

5. Set weekly goals.

Rehearsal I

Goal: overview of the piece and positive response from the choir

Procedure

1. Let the children hear the piece; use instruments or sing it. This could take place before they see the music; involve them in discussing their general impression: "What did you notice about this music?" Guide the children to specific comments about tempo, dynamics, and mood.

2. Introduce some element of the piece through a warm-up activity of some kind. This could take the form of echo-clapping in the meter of the piece or singing a recurring melodic pattern on a neutral syllable. Perhaps there is a refrain that could be learned quickly.

3. Distribute the music and have the children listen to it again or to part of it if it is long. Make sure they know which of the staves they are to follow. Sometimes it is helpful for the singers to mark their parts with a highlighter pen.

4. Sing it straight through, helping them listen for the melody. Reinforcement from the piano will be needed.

Rehearsal II

Goal: one section learned well, note accuracy, minimum accompaniment

Procedure

1. Present games, reading exercises, vocalises related to the piece. Motives or phrases may be extracted for reading activities (rhythmic and/or melodic). Vocal difficulties such as troublesome consonants may suggest specific exercises.

2. Work on melody and words, separately and together. Correct mistakes consistently. Sometimes children need to focus on one element, such as the text itself, or the rhythm of the text, or the melody itself. Speak the text without, and then with, the correct rhythm. Then practice the melody without the text before combining them.

3. Point out expressive elements; do not postpone all interpretation. These considerations will be a continuing concern, but obvious dynamic, articulation, or tempo markings should not be ignored for any length of time.

4. Try to do this section without music or with as little as possible. Memory games help. The text may be written on sentence strip (available at school supply stores) in phrases. Mix these up and let

the children put them in the correct order. Or post them on the wall, and remove one at a time until the text is completely memorized.

5. Use accompaniment sparingly; focus on correct singing and careful listening. The piano is useful to provide a sense of the tonality and to support the melody as needed. The accompaniment as embellishment or color is important at a later stage of preparation.

Rehearsal III

Goal: first section memorized and introduction to rest of piece

Procedure

1. Review and memorize portion learned in Rehearsal II. Can someone say (sing?) the words without looking?

2. Work on next section. Similar techniques may be employed (games, exercises, and the like as described above).

3. Sing both sections, polishing section one. Now is the time to attend carefully to expressive qualities, particularly if the two sections have contrasting characters.

4. Use accompaniment carefully, as support. If the accompaniment is independent of the vocal line or has an interesting character of its own, have the singers listen to it, so that they will appreciate it for its own contribution to the piece and to minimize any confusion it may cause.

Rehearsal IV

Goal: other sections or second part learned, full keyboard part added

Procedure

1. Work on any new material, such as the alto part, descant, or coda. Everyone can sing this at first.

2. Put the two parts together without accompaniment. Piano is used for support if needed. Sometimes it is helpful for the director to sing one of the parts while the choir sings the other, in order for the children to get an accurate impression of the combined parts.

3. Continue to polish first two sections.

Rehearsal V

Goal: final preparation, complete accompaniment

Procedure

1. Sing through the entire piece with accompaniment, stopping only if there is a major problem.

2. Ask for small groups to sing sections while others listen. The object is not competition but focused listening and self-evaluation by the singers.

3. Give final reminders about diction, dynamics, and breathing.

4. Add any other accompanying instruments.

5. Make an audio tape. Let the choir listen. Evaluate. Children, like their elders, are naturally curious about their performance, and the objective "testimony" of the tape recorder can often clarify certain artistic points better than the director's comments.

Final Rehearsal Before Performance

Rehearse in the sanctuary or wherever the singers will be, with all participants, and at least once without stopping to correct mistakes.

SAMPLE REHEARSAL SCHEDULE

Example 7.1

Shepherds Awake

Unison voices with keyboard (or handbells) and optional flute

Words and Music
Michael Jothen

Light and dance-like (♩. = 112)

Flute*

If flute is not available, keyboard or bells should play flute part.

Voices

Shep-herds a - wake, rise up this morn; in Beth - le - hem a babe is born!

cresc. poco a poco

Shep-herds a - wake, rise up this morn; in Beth - le - hem a babe is born!

cresc. poco a poco

-man - u - el!   Je - sus is born! Em - man - u -

decresc.

decresc.

-el

f

Shep-herds a - wake, rise up this morn; go and see this babe who's born!

cresc. poco a poco

Shep-herds a - wake, rise up this morn; go and see this babe who's born!

cresc. poco a poco

Je - sus is born! Em - man - u - el! Je - sus is born! Em - man - u -

-el! _____ Em - man - u - el! _____ Em-

(If no flute, piano play flute part and left hand.)

-man - u - el!   Je - sus is born! Em - man - u -

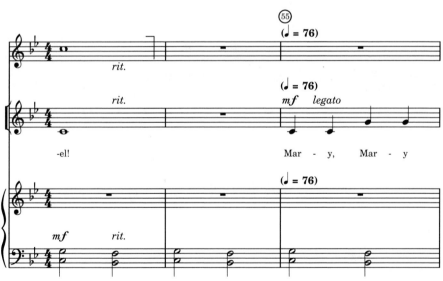

-el!   Mar - y,   Mar - y

watch-ing o'er the ba - by,　Sleep, Em - man - u - el.

Cat - tle　low - ing　'round the man - ger,　Sleep, Em - man - u -

-el.   Sleep, ti - ny ba - by,   Wise Men are com - ing,

com - ing with praise from a - far.   Sleep, ti - ny ba - by,

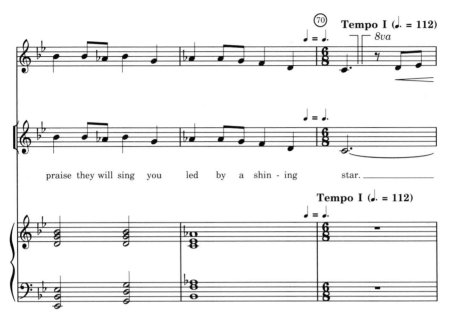

praise they will sing   you   led   by   a   shin - ing   star.

Shep-herds a - wake, rise up   this morn;   the   Son   of   man   to

(If no flute, piano play flute part and left hand to end.)

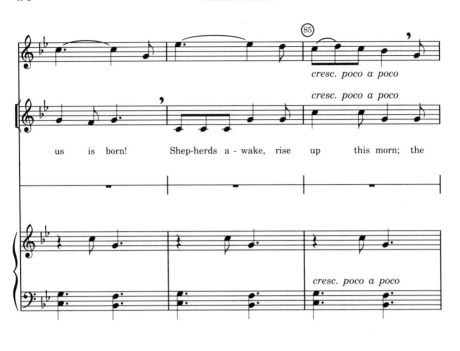

cresc. poco a poco

cresc. poco a poco

us is born! Shep-herds a - wake, rise up this morn; the

cresc. poco a poco

Son of man to us is born! Je - sus is born! Em -

-man - u - el! Je - sus is born! Em - man - u -

-el!

Note: *Suggested tambourine and glockenspiel parts are by Shirley McRae and are given with the permission of the composer.*

Published by Choristers Guild: CGA A-234. Used by permission.

Musical Concepts: $\frac{6}{8}$ meter; Dorian mode (transposed); dynamic contrasts; musical form A A B A; ostinato; texture; legato, marcato

Theological Focus: the visit of the shepherds and the wise men to the manger

Enrichment: Jesus as a shepherd; Epiphany symbols and color.

Words for Study: Epiphany, Emmanuel, musical terms in the piece

Alterations in the Music: addition of tambourine, glockenspiels

Anticipated Musical Problems

1. intonation, especially in the leaps of fourths and fifths and the A naturals of the Dorian mode (transposed)
2. explosive consonants in "awake," "asleep"
3. breath control on extended holds; sustain vowels here
4. control of dynamic contrasts
5. unexpected rest in measure 60
6. word pattern to assist tambourine player

Cautions for the Conductor

1. cues to various instruments
2. tempo and meter changes
3. helping children through extended holds

Rehearsal I

Goals: to develop a feel for the buoyant rhythm and the bright Dorian melody and to experience the melody of the A section

Preparation: Meter

• Listen to the drum.

Example 7.2

- Who can move (skip or gallop) across the room with my drum? (Several try.)
- From a visual, read the text.

  "Shepherds awake, rise up this morn; in Bethlehem a babe is born!"

- Show how it matches drum pattern.
- Clap the phrase.
- Clap it while I play the melody on the recorder (or piano). Does it fit?
- Do it twice. Does my melody change or stay the same?

Preparation: Melody

- Echo sing in C minor (transposed Dorian); include some of the fourths and fifths: use a neutral syllable and $\frac{6}{8}$ meter.
- Show a visual.

Example 7.3

- Echo *after* I sing and point.
- Make up little motives from the scale.

Example 7.4

- Focus on the red notes in the first example (marked above with *) to prepare for these intervals in the melody itself.

Example 7.5

- Sing melody of the first half-phrase.

Example 7.6

- Add rest of the phrase.

The Music

- See how quickly you can find this phrase in the music (measures 9–12).
- Sing it from the music two times without accompaniment (measures 9–16).
- I'll sing the next phrase (measures 17–21).
- Look at measures 33–40; find the phrase again. How has it changed?
- Likewise, beginning with measure 80.
- Stress *k* in awake. What is the word without this consonant?
- Invent a speech exercise with the *k* sound; keep it rhythmic.

Example 7.7

K   K   K   K   a - wake,   a - wake

Rehearsal II

Goals: to finalize melody of A section and sing it musically, no accompaniment as yet

- Who knows the words to this phrase (I clap it)?

Example 7.8

- Here's the melody again. Now sing it; try it from memory.
- Now clap this phrase:

Example 7.9

- Clap it *ff*; *pp*.
- Add words; melody (measures 17–21).
- Learn melody of the "call": *Emmanuel*.
- Read through A A of the piece, noting minor changes; emphasize dynamics always.
- Use only light accompaniment, if any; reinforce melody when needed; try it from memory.

Rehearsal III

Goals: to reinforce A section, memorized, and learn B; to relate to Bible story and Epiphany season

Bible Reference: Have someone read Epiphany story (Matthew 2:1–12). Explain that "Emmanuel" is a Hebrew word meaning "God with us" and is another name for the Christ Child.

Enrichment: Show symbols for Epiphany: the star of Bethlehem, three crowns.

Meter Preparation

- Here's a new pattern.

Example 7.10

- Who can walk to this pattern?
- Have one group of several children move to the $\frac{6}{8}$ rhythm of the A section and one to the $\frac{4}{4}$ rhythm above, alternating turns.

The Music

- Add words to the $\frac{4}{4}$ rhythmic phrase above ("Mary, Mary, watching o'er the baby").
- Contrast with mood and meter of A section.

- Find it in the music (beginning on measure 55).
- Sing this, I'll finish the phrase ("sleep, Emmanuel").
- Compare with the second phrase; snap fingers in the rest. ($\natural$)
- Learn the rest of B section (measures 63–71); add speech to the melody; listen for accuracy of the A♭.
- Go through entire piece; point out the form: A A B A.
- Use accompaniment when possible.

Rehearsal IV

Goals: to memorize entire piece; to add keyboard accompaniment and percussion

- Review song, stopping in the middle of phrases. Who can finish without looking at the music?
- Add keyboard accompaniment.
- Add tambourine, by rote; use word pattern if needed ("Shepherds awake, rise up this morn").
- Add glockenspiel from notation (a visual aid); notice that it is an echo.

Rehearsal V

Goal: to polish the anthem, attending to diction, phrasing, and expressive elements

- Add flute.
- Complete the preparation, with attention to all performance aspects.
- Perform from memory.

SUMMARY

Successful rehearsing means that the children progress in their musical growth and find joy and satisfaction in the experience. Whether or not this happens depends in large measure upon the way the director approaches the task. It is helpful to set realistic objectives and, if possible, communicate them to the children. The director must know all materials thoroughly, be prepared to explain parts of the text, and have strategies for dealing with musical or vocal problems. A written lesson plan or rehearsal agenda makes for more efficient use of time and smoother pacing. Nevertheless, the response of the children may indicate a departure from the plan; the director needs to be sensitive to this and willing to make on-the-spot adjustments. Children love repetition, and there should always be familiar items on the agenda; but surprises are fun, too. Something new, however trivial, adds interest to each rehearsal. A fairly consistent structure, but with some variety, is a good policy. The director is primarily a communicator and should use gestures, facial expression, and body language as well as words. A friendly, positive outlook, high expectations, and a variety of teaching strategies will help keep discipline problems to a minimum. In the long run, children want to be a part of something important and successful, and the dedication of the director inspires this positive response.

CHAPTER 8

Enriching the Program

"Plant a seed before the sense of wonder has been dulled
and self-consciousness imprisons the child."
—RUTH K. JACOBS

Much has been said in this book about the importance of the early childhood years in developing skills and attitudes that may be of lifelong value. So much of an adult's personality, tastes, and achievements is somehow set in motion early in life. While the experiences themselves may be long-forgotten, fundamental feelings about music and one's own musicality persist. If the early experiences have been meager or negative, then the adult is likely to avoid any contacts with the art other than of the most superficial and incidental kind.

On the other hand, stimulating and rewarding activities in music encourage young children and lead them into further exploration and study. Such youngsters become music-loving adults, confident and committed to making music an indispensable part of their lives. Choral experiences provide opportunities to develop not only as singers but also as total musicians who enjoy making music together. The satisfying social aspect of musical ensembles cannot be overlooked, especially for the child whose only other contact with the art is private instruction. The church choir adds a further dimension, a sense of purpose and opportunities for service and leadership in worship. The children may grow in their understanding of God and as functioning members of the church.

A comprehensive choir program will integrate the conventional study of liturgical materials and rudiments of music with special activities designed to enrich the choral experience. These can add variety, zest, and depth to the program and complement the routine aspects of rehearsing. This chapter will suggest a number of ways to do this. Some of the activities may be included in the rehearsal period itself; others involve additional time.

SPECIAL STUDIES

Once or twice during the choir year, there may be a special topic to be studied, with puzzles, games, and workbook pages to be incorporated into the rehearsal or as take-home activities. Only five or ten minutes of the rehearsal itself need be devoted to a given topic, which may be spread out over a month or more. Time before and after rehearsal may be used to advantage as well. Suggested topics and several sample workbook pages are provided here. Refer to Appendix B for resource materials.

Symbolism

The Christian tradition abounds with symbols, which, unlike pictures, are simply suggestions (visual, in this case) of events, ideas, or people. Older children understand the concept of symbols, which we use as directions in much of everyday life. Symbols circumvent the problems of language and literacy as well as, in the case of church design and decoration, adding beauty to the environment. A sample outline follows describing a four-week study of symbolism.

The purpose of this study is to introduce some of the historic symbols of the Christian faith in order to bring about deeper spiritual experiences in worship.

1. The Cross

This is the chief symbol of the Christian church because it reminds us of Christ's sacrifice. There are more than 400 forms of the cross. Simple posters may be made to illustrate some of the commonest forms. Suggestions:

a. Latin cross
b. Graded, or Calvary, cross
c. St. Andrew's cross
d. Greek cross

e. Celtic, or Ionic, cross
f. Maltese cross
g. Papal cross
h. Russian cross

2. Symbols of the Apostles

Most of the traditional symbols of the Apostles indicate the manner in which they died. Since these symbols are frequently used in church decoration, a visit to churches in which they are used would be helpful.

3. Colors and the Christian Year

This subject is suitable for a special unit of its own, but since color is an important symbol in itself, it is appropriate to include it here as well. The colors of the church paraments reflect specific seasons or events in the

Christian Year. Activities: (1) a tour of area churches to see examples of the symbols studied, (2) felt banners created by the children featuring selected symbols, (3) workbook pages, puzzles, drawings to color.

4. Symbols of Doctrine

This lesson may include any symbols not specifically mentioned in other lessons. Such symbols have, through the centuries, helped to proclaim the faith. Suggestions include:

a. Circle
b. Rose
c. Anchor
d. Pointed Arch

e. Pomegranate
f. Wheat
g. Grapes
h. Butterfly

i. Lamp
j. Shield of David (in Jewish symbolism represents God. The six points of the star signify power, majesty, wisdom, love, mercy, and justice.)

See chapter appendix for a sample worksheet.

Religious Art and Architecture

Religion has inspired not only fine music but also paintings, sculpture, and architecture of incomparable beauty. Churches often house some of these works or are themselves superb examples of artistry and workmanship. The purpose of this study is to increase awareness of church design and an appreciation of great religious art.

1. Art

a. Sculpture
b. Paintings
c. Murals

d. Tapestries
e. Stained-glass windows

2. Architecture

a. The steeple and the bell
b. The sanctuary: Akron, or pulpit-centered, and Cruciform, or divided chancel
c. The altar, the pulpit, and the lectern

The Hymnal

The children's choir provides a logical opportunity to learn about the church's primary source of music and poetry. An appreciation for great hymns of all periods of the church's history and a working knowledge of the hymnal itself will be of lifelong value to the child. Many active church members are woefully ignorant of the mechanics of the book and sometimes of the hymnody itself. The purpose of this study, then, is to acquaint the child with representative hymns and the indexes and other aids to worship.

The following generic outline may be adapted to individual hymnals.

1. Organization of the book: indicated by the table of contents
   a. What kinds of materials are included?
   b. How can these materials be found?

Activity: children practice locating sections and indexes listed in the table of contents.

2. The hymns: two or three hymns of different styles and character
   a. Sing the hymns, discuss their meaning.
   b. Provide any interesting background information.
   c. Note other information provided with the hymn: Scriptural basis, tune name, meter, author, and composer or source of tune; explain the hymn format.

Activity: workbook pages giving information about specific hymns and their writers; make a tape recording of several favorite hymns.

3. The indexes: what purposes they serve
   a. Index by Titles
   b. Index by First Lines
   c. Metrical Index
   d. Topical Index
   e. Index of Tune Names
   f. Index of Composers, Authors, and Sources
   g. Index of Scripture References of Hymns
   h. Index to Other Aids to Worship

Activity: children practice locating hymns by means of the various indexes (for example, Who can find a hymn by Martin Luther?). See also the sample workbook pages found in the appendix for this chapter.

4. Other worship materials: lectionary, rituals, service music, prayers, psalter activity. Have children find these materials in the hymnal.

Composers and Hymn Writers

A survey of well-known composers and prominent poets is one way to approach this subject. Children are often surprised to see a hymn by a composer whom they know through their study of the piano or other instrument. Another idea is to concentrate on a single composer, such as Beethoven. Activities may center around his life, a hymn such as "Joyful, Joyful, We Adore Thee," and his other music, and culminate in a birthday party on or around December 16.[1] Another activity is to compose a tune for a given text or to write additional stanzas for some simple children's hymn.

The Pipe Organ

This study is valuable whether or not the church owns such an instrument. General information would include the structure and the history of the pipe organ and how it works. The children should be given a demonstration of the variety of sounds the organ can create, visiting another church or two if need be. If possible, they should see the pipe chambers as well. Attending an organ recital is another appropriate activity. Refer to Appendix B for resources. A suggested outline and worksheet are found on pp. 205–207.

Instruments in the Church

The variety of instruments mentioned in the Bible, especially those associated with Hebrew worship, makes possible an enriching study for the choristers. Ancient instruments such as the sistrum, the timbrel, and the lyre are interesting; but the more familiar trumpet, harp, cymbal, lute, and flute are also Biblical. Drawings for the children to color and include in their workbooks will provide take-home activities. Scripture readings that mention these instruments may be included in the rehearsal. Other instruments commonly used in worship—piano, organ, violin, and recorder—may be included as well.

The Christian Year

The seasons of the Christian Year serve to remind the congregation of the life and ministry of Jesus as well as various aspects of the Christian life. Symbols, colors, and hymns associated with the various seasons may be used. Curtis Werdal describes a clever project that presents the seasons in the form of a road trip that takes place on the church parking lot.[2] Another presentation that continues throughout the choir season is described on pp. 208–209.

INDIVIDUAL ACTIVITIES

Workbooks

The use of choir workbooks is a valuable way to achieve continuity between rehearsals, in that the children have materials to take home and activities

---

[1]There is an extended study of Mozart—"Wolfgang Amadeus Mozart: Wonder Child" by J. Kenneth Robinson—in the October 1986 issue of *Choristers Guild Letters.*

[2]See "Road Trip Around the Christian Year," *Choristers Guild Letters,* April 1987, 194–195.

to carry on outside the rehearsal itself. Furthermore, they are tangible reminders that each child has a contribution to make. Stickers can be placed on pages as awards, new materials can be added regularly, and the choristers themselves may decorate their workbooks individually. In essence, the use of workbooks sends a message that choir is important and what goes on there is worth remembering.

Choir workbooks may be organized in a variety of ways and may be prepared before the choir season begins. However, children enjoy adding pages throughout the year rather than being presented with a complete package at the beginning. Possible workbook materials are as follows:

a. Description of the merit system: what it consists of and requirements for awards. Any kind of point system should be clearly defined.
b. Overview of the year's activities, with dates, if possible
c. Chorister's pledge, creed, or prayer
d. Names of choristers, with birthdays and phone numbers
e. Special study pages
f. Liturgies used in the worship service, and perhaps a service bulletin
g. Kodály (Curwen) hand signals (see page 68)
h. Puzzles, drawings to color
i. List of hymns and anthems to be learned
j. Prayers: before rehearsal, meals, sleep
k. List of musical terms
l. Awards: Some directors give simple certificates from time to time—weekly, even—for some achievement.
m. Cartoons or diagrams illustrating some vocal principle (good posture, singing or speaking voice)

Puzzles

Children of all ages enjoy gamelike activities, and carefully constructed puzzles can reinforce musical concepts from rehearsal. Sample pages are found in the chapter appendix.

Contests

As long as the competitive aspect is not overemphasized, occasional contests are an additional incentive to the children. Hymn-memorizing contests have been successful, the children learning the first stanza of hymns from a list provided by the director. Choir assistants are useful for this, to hear the children before or after rehearsal. An award, such as a hymnal, may be presented to a single winner or to all children who memorize a prescribed number of hymns. This contest can be a yearlong venture. Awards may also be given for attendance or for bringing new members to the choir. Weekly awards (who maintains the best posture today?) are simple incentives for individual cooperation and achievement.

Games

Some directors have games and small group activities for the children as they gather for rehearsal.[3] Memorization games may save time in rehearsal. Present phrases (in scrambled form) from a hymn or anthem that the children are learning. These may be done on workbook pages or as a small group activity with each child receiving one phrase on a card. The object is to see how quickly they can arrange the phrases in the correct order.

COMMUNITY SERVICE AND NONLITURGICAL PERFORMANCES

The regular choir performance schedule can be enriched by extending the services to the community. The appearance of a well-prepared children's choir brings joy to residents of nursing or retirement homes, for example, and emphasizes the value of giving pleasure to others. Further outreach events would include singing at other churches, in parks, or for community gatherings. Such activities often result in new members for the choir, too.

Many children's choirs enjoy presenting a musical during the season, although there is much additional time and preparation involved. Musicals are often based on Biblical stories and involve staging and costumes as well as music and dialogue. There are a number of these on the market; one should take care to choose one that has real musical value and to maintain the same vocal standards as in the regular choral pursuits. Some imaginative directors create, with the help of the children, original productions based on songs or stories. One appropriate story is "The Legend of Old Befana," an Italian Christmas tale (see Appendix C).

Mary Ellen Pinzino describes a wonderful Renaissance musical presentation produced by a children's chorus.[4]

---

[3]See Jo Ann Butler's ideas—"Twenty-Two Activities for Teaching Music Facts"—in *Choristers Guild Letters,* September, October, and November 1983, 2–6, 47–49, and 61–63.

[4]See "Mini Madrigal Feast," in *Choristers Guild Letters,* September 1985, 5–6, for details of this Christmas event involving singing, recorders, juggling, mime, fencing, and a variety of crafts, as well as the customary wassail and plum pudding.

INSTRUMENTAL GROUPS

A choral program may inspire some children to pursue additional musical activities. If there is sufficient interest and if leadership is available, certain instrumental ensembles may be organized to complement the choir experience. It is well known that instrumental study expedites musical literacy, and the satisfaction derived from such small ensemble work is great indeed.

Many churches support handbell choirs for a variety of age groups. While there is considerable expense involved at the outset, the unique appeal of the handbell sound and the availability of handbells to all sectors of the congregation tend to make such a purchase worthwhile. Some amateur groups perform with impeccable precision and polish. There is a wide selection of handbell literature and a number of choral anthems with handbell accompaniments.

The recorder is enjoying renewed popularity, as reflected in professional groups and as an educational tool in elementary schools. Unlike handbells or Orff instruments, the recorder is inexpensive, with instruments of good quality being generally affordable. Furthermore, there is a wealth of easy ensemble literature, making satisfying group playing possible for beginners.

If attempts to integrate Orff experiences into regular rehearsals becomes frustrating, an Orff percussion ensemble might be the solution. Even under the best of circumstances, there is not enough time for all the children to become proficient in playing the instruments. A separate group is the obvious way to develop technique and to experience exciting ensemble music. Both unpitched and barred percussion may be used in instrumental arrangements and accompaniments for anthems.

FESTIVALS AND SUMMER EVENTS

Choir festivals for children are rapidly increasing in popularity, due to the combined efforts of dedicated directors who seek for their singers an inspiring and exciting musical experience beyond the church choir itself. Anyone who has ever participated in a massed choir knows the thrill it affords. For children it can be a goal, an incentive, and an opportunity to sing with other choirs that have worked toward this same goal. For the small choir, the sheer beauty of the sound is a revelation. It also gives some choirs the opportunity to perform music that might otherwise be beyond their reach, although music chosen should be generally usable by all participating choirs.

A children's choir festival is usually a weekend event featuring area choirs in a concert of music that has been learned by all participating groups. After a day of rehearsing and other activities (small group workshops, crafts, refreshments) the concert or worship service usually takes place the following day. Many festivals are ecumenical in nature, under the auspices of a group such as the Choristers Guild local chapter. Working with choirs of many denominations in a shared musical experience can be an inspiring introduction for the children into the inclusive Christian family. The director for the occasion can be one of the local musicians or an invited guest, usually someone with known interest and expertise in children's choirs.

The key to a successful festival is organization. Preparations should begin many months before the actual event. A committee representing all anticipated groups selects the director, an accompanist, and a date and location. After these initial decisions, certain considerations must be discussed.

1. Age range. Grades 3–6, or 4–6, are usually compatible. Grades 4–8 is the maximum range.
2. Initial contacts. Area churches need to be informed as soon as the date and place are decided.
3. Fee. There is usually some charge assessed to participating choirs to cover expenses for the event.
4. Theme. This is not necessary, but some groups like to plan around a theme, which may then be carried out in publicity, program covers, and banners.
5. Music. The musical director of the festival usually likes to be consulted in this matter, although the local committee may make the initial selections. Music should reflect a variety of styles, moods, and texts and be within the capabilities of participating choirs. One or two of the selections could be fairly complex or require resources beyond the reach of smaller churches—such is part of the excitement of festival music. But there will be greater participation if most of the music is also usable during the year by individual choirs. To summarize, music selection is best made by local committees in consultation with the chosen director.
6. Music interpretation. If the director is a resident of the area, a meeting early in the year to discuss the music is advisable. By whatever method, however, certain aspects of performance need to be agreed upon so that all choirs will learn the music in generally the same way. Important points such as tempo, descants, key changes, or any other alterations in the score need to be decided. If the accompaniment calls for instrumentalists other than the organist, these persons need to be contacted.

7. Memorizing. Will the choristers be required to memorize their music? Will children who are unprepared be permitted to sing? Is attendance at the general rehearsal required?

8. Subcommittees. Even a small event entails numerous administrative tasks that need to be distributed among committee members. A publicity chairman is essential. This person sends out all notices to churches, makes contacts with local media, takes pictures of the choir, and maintains a publicity file for future festivals. If the event is to be recorded, someone needs to be assigned this responsibility. Other aspects of the festival to be covered are food (lunch or refreshments on rehearsal day); logistics (registering the children, assembling them before the festival, seating arrangements, processional); decoration (banners, flowers); programs and seating (special section for parents, directors); finances (receive fees and pay all bills).

9. Evaluation. Immediately after the festival the committee should evaluate the event in all its aspects, recording in detail all comments, positive and negative. This is the prime time for receiving suggestions for improvement. It is also a good time to appoint a chairman for the next year's festival.

Some churches sponsor summer choir events, operated along the line of vacation church school. Sometimes these are regional in scope, held at a residential camp in the area. In general, they provide opportunity for fairly intensive musical instruction, along with worship, crafts, recreation music, and the like.[5]

SPECIAL SERVICES

From time to time, certain occasions in the life of a church will inspire special celebration, and the children's choir may well participate in these. Jeanne S. Fogle in *Choristers Guild Letters,* August 1986, describes an All Saints' Day service in which deceased church members were commemorated. The children processed, carrying banners memorializing the honored members. Pentecost Sunday is another festive occasion that is often celebrated on a grand scale, involving children.

In addition to liturgical occasions, many churches plan simple ceremonies honoring their choirs. One of these is the dedication service, usually included in a worship service at the beginning of the choir season. Actually,

---

[5]For descriptions of successful ventures of this type, see "Worshipping God Our Creator," by Micky Cloud *(Choristers Guild Letters,* April 1988, 201–202), and "Now Is the Time to Start Planning for Your Vacation Choir School," by Barbara Gulick *(Choristers Guild Letters,* February 1987, 154–155).

the entire service, including hymns and readings, may relate to the musical theme. Components of such a service may be as follows:

1. Presentation of the choirs. Choirs may be seated in front pews or may assemble in the front of the sanctuary.
2. Pledge. This may be in the form of a litany or a series of questions put to the choirs by the minister in which they affirm their commitment to serve God and the church with energy, love, and faithfulness through the choir. The congregation may likewise be called to support the choirs through encouragement and attendance at worship.
3. Prayers or collects. These may express thankfulness for music, glorification of God through hymns and anthems, and dedication of time and talent to service.
4. Blessing—some kind of statement of faith and affirmation from the minister to the choirs
5. Scripture—one or more readings pertaining to music
6. Hymns reflecting praise, joy, singing in worship ("When in Our Music God Is Glorified," "I Sing the Almighty Power of God," "Come, Christians, Join to Sing," for example)

At the conclusion of the choir year, a recognition service may be held to honor the choirs for their faithful contributions to the worship life of the church. In addition to special prayers, readings, and hymns (as in the dedication service described above), other elements may be included:

1. Recognition of individual choirs; presentation of certificates
2. Recognition of individual children for special awards (pins, certificates, hymnals)
3. Each choir may sing an anthem, or a special combined choir anthem may be sung.

In education circles, one hears the term "closure" used to indicate the pulling together, the synthesizing of the activities in a given lesson. Choir members likewise benefit from a satisfying conclusion to a season of stewardship and hard work. Simple affirmation by minister and congregation brings the music program into focus and elevates the musicians to their well-earned position of honor. As we have seen, music and worship from Old Testament times have been inextricably bound in the religious expression of God's people, adult and child alike. And as for the future,

> When we've been there ten thousand years,
> Bright shining as the sun,
> We've no less days to sing God's praise
> Than when we'd first begun.
> ("Amazing Grace")

Christmas Symbols

 Lighted Candle   Symbolizes Christ as the light of the world. According to an old legend, lighted candles placed in the window guided the Christ child in his wanderings on Christmas Eve.

Lighted Lamp   Symbol of the word of God

 Blossoming Rose   Symbol of Advent

Star of Epiphany   Commemorates the visit of the Magi

Christmas Tree   Symbol of Christ as the Tree of Life. In the 10th century a beautiful legend began to spread all through Europe. According to the story, on the night Christ was born, all the trees in the wood, even those in the ice and snow, bloomed and bore fruit.

Laurel, Holly, and Ivy   In ancient Rome, laurel was the emblem of peace, joy, and victory. Holly and ivy take a place in Christian homes to show that Christ has come in.

Yule Log   The custom of the Druids was to light fires in the Yule season to burn out the sins and evil of the past year. In early Christian times, the log became a part of Christmas celebration, representing Christ, Light of the World.

 Bells   In medieval times bells were tolled on Christmas Eve to warn the powers of darkness of the coming of the Savior. It was believed that "the Devil died when Christ was born."

A Trip Through the Hymnal

See how long this trip takes. Time yourself!

Beginning_____ Finish time_____

Total time for the trip_____

How many hymns are there all together?_____

What is the title of the first hymn in the hymnal?_____

_____

Who wrote the text (the words)?_____

Find a hymn tune named for a saint_____ or street_____

For a city or town_____

How many hymns are in Short Meter (66.86)?_____

Name one hymn tune in 87.87.87 meter. _____

Suppose you wanted to find a hymn for Epiphany. Which index would you

use?_____

Most people find a hymn by its title or first line. Find the index for this
and write down the number of the following hymns.

     "For the Beauty of the Earth"_____
     "All Creatures of Our God and King"_____
     "O Come, All Ye Faithful"_____
     "Amazing Grace"_____

Trivia

How many hymns begin with "O"?_____

How many hymns were written by Isaac Watts?_____

How many stanzas long is "O God, Our Help in Ages Past"?_____

If you sing all the stanzas of "All Creatures of Our God and King," how

many times do you sing "Alleluia"?_____

What is your favorite hymn?_____

What is its number in the hymnal?_____

Word Search

The hymn, "All Things Bright and Beautiful" mentions ten things that God has created. Can you find them in the puzzle below? They may be read across, up, down, backward, or diagonally.

```
M   T   D   R   I   B   C   O   S
M   O   R   N   I   N   G   E   U
B   F   U   K   L   S   R   P   N
J   L   H   N   B   U   F   D   S
W   O   Z   K   T   N   R   L   E
R   W   B   A   M   A   U   W   T
S   E   E   O   R   B   I   I   A
F   R   I   V   E   R   T   N   L
C   T   B   A   N   G   S   D   K
```

These are the words: river wind sun sunset morning fruits creatures flower bird mountain

Find the Picture in the Puzzle

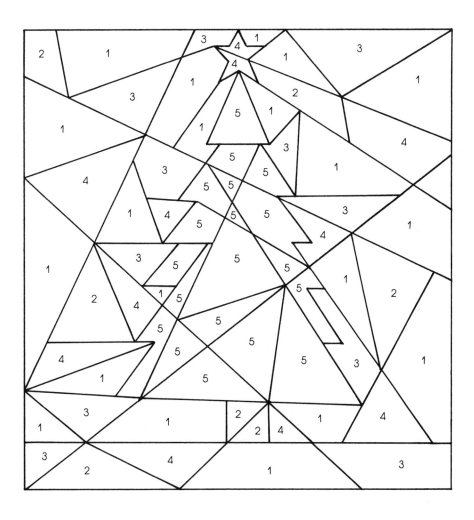

Color in each section to find the picture hidden in the puzzle. Figure out what color each number stands for by looking up each hymn. The color is mentioned in the stanza listed with each hymn.

_____	1	"This Is My Father's World" (Stanza 2)
_____	2	"All Things Bright and Beautiful" (Stanza 2)
_____	3	"Come Ye Faithful, Raise the Strain" (Stanza 1)
_____	4	"It Came Upon a Midnight Clear" (Stanza 1)
_____	5	"The Lord Is My Shepherd" (Stanza 1)

—Martha Israel, used by permission

Hymn Square

A	S	L	P	L	V	T	W	H	Y	I	F	N
O	G	U	S	B	W	N	I	L	S	W	E	K
A	I	N	P	D	Q	W	A	O	P	N	R	D
T	E	M	R	H	F	Y	U	E	L	S	T	M
H	D	E	C	L	B	O	H	R	J	D	L	G
R	O	S	D	F	M	C	A	L	D	T	E	A
T	N	H	J	E	V	M	S	A	O	L	F	L

Begin ↗

Color in every *other* square to find a phrase from one of the hymns we are learning this month. Write the phrase here: _____

What hymn is it from? _____

What page is it on in our hymnal? _____

Break the Code

Z	S	H			I	G		D	F	O	W	G	S		U	C	R

K	W	H	V		C	I	F		G	W	B	U	W	B	U

There is a secret message above.

Break the code to find it! Each letter in the outside ring stands for the letter in front of it on the inside ring.

Write the letters in the boxes beneath the code letters at the top of the page.

Work the Crossword Puzzle

These are all words that are important to a choir!

ACROSS

2. A group that sings together
4. To repeat a rhythm or melody after the leader
5. A place to keep choir pages
7. Your best musical instrument
8. A choir does this
9. To talk and listen to God
11. Beautiful sounds

DOWN

1. A choir needs to do this
3. The first part of singing
6. This helps us sing correctly
10. A short song of praise to God

The Pipe Organ

Director's Outline: A Four-Week Study

Week One

I. Introduction to the pipe organ
   A. What is a pipe organ?
      1. Keyboard instrument
      2. Wind instrument
      3. Church instrument
      4. Rock instrument (electronic)
   B. Where is it located in our church?
   C. When is it used, and for what?
   D. What do we call the person who plays it?
II. Brief history of the pipe organ
   A. First musical instrument to have a keyboard
   B. "Pipes of Pan" work like organ pipes
   C. Mentioned in the Bible in Genesis 4:21 (Jubal)
   D. Water-powered organ built by Greeks in 146 B.C. (Cicero, Nero)
   E. Bellows organ (wind-powered) in fourth century (Constantinople)
   F. Bach, a very important organist
   G. Oldest existing playable organ in Sion, Switzerland, built in 1390
   H. Nickname is "The King of Instruments"
III. General information
   A. Look at several pictures of pipe organs and find:
      1. The console (keyboard part)
      2. The pipes
   B. What happens when a key is played?
      1. Blower fills chest with air (find blower and wind-chest)
      2. Organist pushes key down
         a. Pulls lever between wind-chest and pipe down
         b. Air from wind-chest goes up into pipe causing it to sound

Week Two: The Pipes

I. Look at actual pipes (or "toy flute" and "Halloween horn").
II. Talk about the differences in sound.
III. Different sizes
   A. Longest usually 32 feet
   B. Shortest can be smaller than a pencil
IV. Examine actual pipes, if possible.
   A. Distinguish between wood and metal pipes; pipes of various shapes.

B. Present notebook page.
V. Difference between two basic types of pipes
    A. Flue pipes
    B. Reed pipes
VI. Listen to actual pipe families, or recordings.

Week Three: The Console

I. Review pipe terms from week two.
II. Introduce new terms:

blower	rank
console	reed pipes
division	reservoir
expression shades	scale (relation of a pipe's
flue pipes	length to its diameter)
manual	specification
mixtures	stop
pedal	wind-chest
pitch	

III. Demonstrate parts of the console on church organ, if possible.

Week Four: The Organist

I. Discuss the various duties of the organist: improvise, lead choir (in some cases), introduce and accompany hymns, play for weddings and funerals.
II. Suggested activities
    A. Ask the children to pretend to play a familiar tune with their feet.
    B. Let the children actually play the organ.
    C. Let the children see the pipe chambers (in small groups).
    D. Look at the church bulletin and underline all the parts of the service that the organist plays.
        1. What is a prelude?
        2. What is an offertory?
        3. What is a postlude?
    E. Find out what other services the organist plays.
        1. Weddings
        2. Funerals
        3. Special services (Christmas Eve, Thanksgiving)
    F. Invite the organist to play for the children.
        1. Demonstrate different organ sounds.
        2. Play next Sunday's prelude, offertory, or postlude.
    G. Attend an organ recital.
    H. Visit other churches and look at and listen to their organs.

—Ellen Koziel, used by permission

Connect the Dots

21 •

20 •

• 19

22 •

• 18

23 •

24 •

• 17
25

Connect the dots from 1 to 25
and find a very important part
of a pipe organ!

1 •

• 16

2 •

• 15

3 •

• 14

4 • •

• 13

5 •

• 12

• 11

6 •

7 •

• 10

8 • • 9

A Children's Choir Study of the Christian Year

The purpose of this study is to help the child appreciate and relive the life and ministry of Jesus Christ in a systematic fashion. The child will also learn to recognize the colors and symbols of each season.

The study is to be presented at one rehearsal each month, starting in November. Activities in each session should require no more than 5–10 minutes of rehearsal time. Preparations should be set up ahead of time and prepared by choir assistants.

I. Late November: ADVENT
   A. Introduce the Christian Year
      1. Bulletin board with Cross and ⊛, signifying the two large divisions of the church year. Names of the seasons are already inserted, but not symbols.
      2. Explain Christian Year:
         a. The festival portion tracing Christ's life and work (Advent to Pentecost)
         b. The nonfestival portion emphasizing the standards of Christian life (season after Pentecost)
   B. Introduce Advent

      1. Definition: "Coming," a four-week period of preparation for the coming of the Lord at Christmas
      2. Color: Purple or blue
      3. Symbols: Candles, rose, wreath
   C. Advent Hymn: Veni Emmanuel—"O Come, O Come, Emmanuel" or Stuttgart— "Come thou long expected Jesus"
   D. Activity: Children bring greenery from home to decorate base of an Advent wreath. Candles will be lit during choir rehearsals in Advent.
II. December: CHRISTMAS
   A. Introduce Christmas
      1. Definition: "Christ's Mass"—Celebrated on December 25 to commemorate Christ's birth
      2. Color: White
      3. Symbols: Angel, manger, wreath
   B. Christmas Hymn: Mendelssohn—"Hark the Herald Angels Sing." Greensleeves—"What Child Is This?"
   C. Activity: Children participate in making an Advent/Christmas banner using symbols studied.
III. January: EPIPHANY
   A. Introduce Epiphany
      1. Definition: The coming of the Magi (Wise Men)
      2. Color: Green
      3. Symbols: Five pointed star, three crowns
   B. Epiphany Hymn: Puer Nobis—"What Star Is This?" or "We Three Kings"

C. Activity: Epiphany puzzle (see p.210)

IV. February: LENT

A. Introduce Lent

    1. Definition: A season commemorating the suffering and death of Jesus; forty days between Ash Wednesday and Easter

    2. Color: Purple—Black on Good Friday

    3. Symbols: Palms, crown of thorns with nails, cross with draped sheet.

B. Lenten Hymn: St. Flavian—"Lord, who throughout these forty days"

C. Activity: Lenten Puzzle (similar to Epiphany Puzzle)

V. March: EASTER

A. Introduce Easter

    1. Definition: The resurrection of Our Lord

    2. Color: White

    3. Symbols: Butterfly, Easter lily, cross and crown

B. Easter Hymn: Easter Hymn—"Jesus Christ Is Risen Today" or Salve Festa Dies—"Hail Thee, Festival Day"

C. Activity: Dye Easter eggs and decorate with Christian symbols; Easter banner.

VI. April: PENTECOST

A. Introduce Pentecost

    1. Definition: "Fiftieth"—Pentecost is the fiftieth day after Easter; it is the day that the Holy Spirit descended upon the Apostles.

    2. Color: Red

    3. Symbols: Tongues of fire, descending dove

B. Pentecost Hymn: Veni Creator—"O Come, Creator Spirit"

C. Activity: Pentecost banner

VII. May: SEASON AFTER PENTECOST

A. Introduce Season after Pentecost

    1. Definition: Longest season of the church year (22–27 Sundays); emphasizes Christian life. It is followed by Advent.

    2. Color: Green

    3. Symbols: Symbols of the Trinity, symbols depicting growth (plant)

B. Hymn: Grand Isle—"I Sing a Song of the Saints of God." Lytlington—"God Be in My Head"

C. Activity: Silent "Symbol Scavenger Hunt": Teams of children move silently around church searching for symbols studied.

—Above outline by Debbie Clifton, used by permission

Epiphany Puzzle

1. Jesus' parents were named _____
   and _____ .

2. Jesus was born in _____ .

3. Three Magi or _____ _____ came to
   visit the Baby Jesus.

4. They were not Jews but were _____ .

5. Their names were _____ , _____ ,
   and _____ .

6. They came bearing gifts of _____ ,
   _____ , and _____ .

7. From which direction did they come? _____ .

Find Your Answers Here:

m (y) rrh   Mary   (J) (o) (s) eph

(E) ast   (G) en (t) ile (s)   g (o) l (d)

Balthazar   Bethl (e) hem   (G) aspar

W (i) (s) e Men   Melchior   (f) (r) anki (n) c (e) ns (e)

For Fun, Unscramble the Circled Letters to Find a Message:

__ __ __ U__ I S __ __ __'__ __ __ __ __

F O R __ V __ __ __ __ __ __

Sample Banners to Be Designed by Children
Simplicity Should Be Stressed

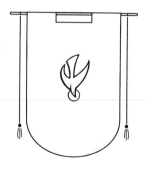

Scrambled Words

Directions:

Unscramble the words below and place them in the correct phrases from one of the anthems we are learning.

ghawtnic   gnlwio   wkaea   apsrei

emiswne   igsn   egramn   robn   gihnsin

1. Shepherds _____, rise up this morn

2. In Bethlehem, a babe is _____

3. Mary, Mary, _____ o'er the baby

4. Cattle _____ 'round the _____

5. Sleep, tiny baby, _____ are coming

6. Coming with _____ from afar

7. Praise they will _____ you led by a _____ star

In the Stars Write the Title of the Anthem:

211

Professional Organizations

American Choral Directors
Association
P.O. Box 6310
Lawton, OK 73506

American Guild of English
Handbell Ringers, Inc.
1055 Centerville Station Road
Dayton, OH 45459

American Guild of Organists
National Headquarters
475 Riverside Dr., Suite 1260
New York, NY 10115

American Orff-Schulwerk
Association
Executive Headquarters
P.O. Box 391089
Cleveland, OH 44139-1089

American Recorder Society
596 Broadway, Suite 902
New York, NY 10012-3234

Americas Boychoir Federation
P.O. Box 677
125 S. Fourth St.
Connellsville, PA 15425

Choristers Guild
2834 W. Kingsley Rd.
Garland, TX 75041

Dalcroze Society of America
Julia Schnebly-Black, President
3871 Forty-Fifth Avenue, NE
Seattle, WA 98105

Hymn Society of America
National Headquarters
Texas Christian University
Fort Worth, TX 76129

Music Educators National
Conference
1902 Association Drive
Reston, VA 22091

National Association of Teachers
of Singing
2800 University Blvd., N.
Jacksonville, FL 32211

Organization of American Kodály
Educators
Department of Music
Nicholls State University
Thibodaux, LA 70301

Royal Canadian College of
Organists
500 University Ave., Suite 614
Toronto, Ontario M5G 1V7

Published Resources

Books for Professional Growth

Choksy, Lois. *The Kodály Context*. Englewood Cliffs, N.J.: Prentice-Hall, 1981. Intended as a companion volume to *The Kodály Method*. An outgrowth of work with teachers in the San Jose School District.

———. *The Kodály Method*. Englewood Cliffs, N.J.: Prentice-Hall, 1974. An introduction to the method in America.

Choksy, Lois, Robert Abramson, Avon Gillespie, and David Woods. *Teaching Music in the Twentieth Century*. Englewood Cliffs, N.J.: Prentice-Hall, 1986. Philosophy and practice of four approaches: Kodály, Dalcroze, Orff, and Comprehensive Musicianship.

Ehmann, Wilhelm, and Frauke Hassemann. *Voice Building for Choirs*. Chapel Hill, NC: Hinshaw Music, 1982. A Westminster Choir College Library selection.

Gardner, Howard. *Art, Mind, and Brain: A Cognitive Approach to Creativity*. New York: Basic Books, 1982. A fascinating study of children's creativity in the arts by a leading cognitive psychologist.

Holt, John. *How Children Learn*. New York: Pitman, 1967. Insights into children and teachers by the late critic of the American educational system.

Ingram, Madeline, and William Rice. *Vocal Techniques for Children and Youth*. Nashville: Abingdon Press, 1962. An older but useful selection.

Jacobs, Ruth K. *The Children's Choir*. Philadelphia: Fortress Press, 1957. Practical ideas and guidance assembled by the founder of the Choristers Guild.

Keetman, Gunild. *Elementaria*. Translated by Margaret Murray. London: Schott, 1974. Fundamental handbook to the Orff Schulwerk by a leading exponent; contains techniques as well as philosophy.

Keller, Wilhelm. *Introduction to Music for Children*. Translated by Susan Kennedy. London: Schott, 1963. Philosophy and practice of the Schulwerk by an eminent educator.

Kemp, Helen. *Of Primary Importance*. Choristers Guild, 1989. Articles that present practical ideas for working with younger choristers; applications to eight anthems.

Kodály, Zoltán. *The Selected Writings*. New York: Boosey and Hawkes, 1974. Insights into the Kodály method by personal writings of its founder.

McDonald, Dorothy T., and Gene M. Simons. *Musical Growth and Development, Birth through Six*. New York: Schirmer Books, 1989. A research-based introduction to the way young children develop musical skills.

Orff, Carl. *The Schulwerk*. London: Schott, 1978. Volume 3 of an eight-volume autobiography by the founder of the Orff Schulwerk; recounts the birth and flowering of the Schulwerk in southern Germany from 1925 to 1950.

Rao, Doreen. *Choral Music Experience*. New York: Boosey and Hawkes, 1987. A collection of twelve booklets featuring topics pertinent to the musical education of the young singer. Repertory and audio-cassette recordings also available.

Roach, Donald. *Handbook for Children's and Youth Choir Directors*. Dallas: Choristers Guild, 1987. Self-help book on organizing and maintaining choirs for children and youth.

Rotermund, Donald, ed. *Children Sing His Praise*. St. Louis: Concordia, 1985. A practical book for children's choir directors contributed by Paul Bouman, Helen Kemp, Carlos Messerli, Ronald Nelson, Donald Rotermund, and David S. Walker.

Swears, Linda. *Teaching the Elementary School Chorus*. West Nyack, NY: Parker Publishing, 1985. A complete guide to building a successful elementary-school chorus.

Books for Enrichment Activities

A. Art and Architecture

Holberton, Paul. *The World of Architecture*. New York: Crescent Books, 1988.

Kessel, Dmitri. *Splendors of Christendom: Great Art and Architecture in European Churches*. Lausanne: Edita, 1964.

Thiry, Paul, Richard M. Bennett, and Henry L. Kamphoefner. *Churches and Temples*. New York: Reinhold, 1952.

B. The Christian Year

Cowie, L. W., and John Selwyn Gummer. *The Christian Calendar*. Springfield, MA: Merriam, 1974.

Horn, Edward T., III. *The Christian Year*. Philadelphia: Fortress Press, 1957.

C. Hymns

Keithahm, Mary Nelson. *Our Heritage of Hymns*. Dallas: Choristers Guild, 1986.

Keithahm, Mary Nelson, and Mary Louis Van Dyke. *Exploring the Hymnal*. Dallas: Choristers Guild, 1986. Companion volume to the above.

Routley, Eric. *A Panorama of Christian Hymnody*. Chicago: G.I.A. Publications, 1981.

Ryden, E. E. *The Story of Christian Hymnody*. Rock Island, IL: Augustana Press, 1959.
Also useful are the companion volumes to denominational hymnals.

D. The Pipe Organ

Barnes, William H. *The Contemporary American Organ*. New York: J. Fischer, 1952. With multiple revisions.
Ochse, Orpha. *The History of the Organ in the United States*. Bloomington and Indianapolis: Indiana University Press, 1975.

E. Symbols of the Christian Church

Bradner, John. *Symbols of the Church Seasons and Days*. Wilton, CT: Morehouse-Barlow, 1977.
Daves, Michael. *Young Reader's Book of Christian Symbolism*. Nashville: Abingdon Press, 1967.
Post, W. Ellwood. *Saints, Signs, and Symbols*. Wilton, CT: Morehouse-Barlow, revised 1974.
West, Canon Edward N. *Outward Signs: The Language of Christian Symbolism*. New York: Walker, 1989.
Wetzler, Robert, and Helen Huntington. *Seasons and Symbols*. Minneapolis: Augsburg Press, 1962.
Whittemore, Carroll E. *Symbols of the Church*. Nashville: Abingdon Press, revised 1988.

Anthem Collections

Alleluia, I Will Sing. Augsburg, 1985. Eight unison or two-part anthems with keyboard accompaniments.
Beck, Theodore, arr. *Sing and Ring*. Augsburg, 1987. Six hymn settings for unison choir, handbells, and organ.
Burke, John T. *W. A. Mozart for Boys and Girls*. Choristers Guild, 1985. One- or two-part settings of Mozart melodies from various sources; new texts.
Easy Anthems for Children's Voices. Broadman Press, 1970. Sixteen unison and two-part easy anthems: general, Thanksgiving, Christmas, and Easter.
Kemp, Helen. *Let's Sing*. Augsburg Fortress, 1988. A collection of songs for young singers compiled by the widely known expert.
Leaf, Robert. *This New Day*. Augsburg, 1976. Five simple unison anthems with keyboard and optional handbells.
Marshall, Jane. *Psalms Together*. Choristers Guild, 1986 and 1988. Six antiphons from the Psalms appearing in the Common Lectionary. Two volumes.
Olson, Howard S., ed. *Lead Us, Lord*. Augsburg, 1977. A collection of African hymns, mostly unison.
O Sing to Our God. Augsburg, 1987. Eight unison anthems with keyboard.
Page, Sue Ellen. *Praise the Lord With Psalms*. Hinshaw Music, 1978. Anthems for treble voices and teaching guides.
Pooler, Marie. *Children's Choir Book, Nine Seasonal Songs*. Augsburg, 1965. Simple unison or two-part anthems for the church year.

Room, Peter. *Carols for Young Voices*. Wise Publishing, 1977. Thirty traditional international Christmas carols; unison, keyboard, melody instruments.

Sing Aloud, Alleluia. Augsburg, 1985. Eight unison, two-part anthems with keyboard, Orff instruments.

Sing Noel. G. Schirmer, 1985. Five Christmas carols, two or three-part treble voices.

Sleeth, Natalie. *Bread and Wine*. Choristers Guild, 1981. Eight vocal pieces for the communion service. Keyboard, guitar, handbells.

Thomas, Paul, ed. *Morning Star Choir Books I, II, III*. Concordia, 1957, 1965, 1970. Standard collections for all occasions.

We Come to Praise Him. Choristers Guild, 1978. Useful collection of easy material for the church year.

Journals

The American Organist. American Guild of Organists, 475 Riverside Drive, Suite 1260, New York, NY 10115.

The Choral Journal. American Choral Directors Association, Box 6310, Lawton, OK 73506.

Choristers Guild Letters. 2834 W. Kingsley Road, Garland, TX 75041.

The Church Music Quarterly. Royal School of Church Music, Addington Palace, Croydon, CR9 5AD, England.

The Diapason. 380 Northwest Highway, Des Plaines, IL 60016.

Kodály Envoy. Nicholls State University, Thibodaux, LA 70301.

Music Educators Journal. 1902 Association Drive, Reston, VA 22091.

The Music Leader. Baptist Sunday School Board, 127 9th Ave. North, Nashville, TN 37234.

Orff Echo. Editorial Office, 332 Gerard Ave., Elkins Park, PA 19117.

Pastoral Music. 225 Sheridan St., NW, Washington, DC 20011.

Children's Hymnals

The Children's Hymnbook. National Union of Christian Schools and William B. Eardmans Publishing Co., 1962.

Church School Hymnal for Children. Philadelphia: Lutheran Church Press, 1964.

Hymns for Primary Worship. Philadelphia: Westminster Press, 1946.

Joyful Sounds. St. Louis: Concordia, 1977. (Grades 6–8)

Little Children Sing to God. St. Louis: Concordia, 1960.

Rejoice and Sing Praise. Nashville: Abingdon, 1977.

Songs of God's Love. St. Louis: Concordia, 1984. (Primary grades)

Songs of Joy. Philadelphia: Fortress Press, 1968.

We Sing of God. Church Hymnal Corporation (Episcopal), 1989. Hymnal, teacher's guide, and worksheet.

Young Children Sing. Minneapolis: Augsburg, 1967.

Canons and Rounds

Bristol, Lee Hastings, Jr. *Thirty-Five Sacred Rounds and Canons from Four Centuries*. Canyon Press, 1955. Simple to moderately difficult; useful collection.

Hall, Doreen. *Canons and Rounds*. Waterloo Music Co., 1982. Speech, movement, rhythmic, and vocal canons. Mostly secular texts.

Lowe, Helenclair. *The Choristers Round Book*. Choristers Guild, 1976. Twenty-eight rounds, sacred and secular, from early American songbooks.

One Hundred and One Rounds for Singing. World Around Songs. Rounds for many occasions.

Rounds for Children. Amsco, 1986. A Division of Music Sales Corporation. Over 100 rounds in 2, 3, and 4 parts; illustrated.

Sacred Canons. World Around Songs, 1963. Sixteen easy canons.

Taylor, Mary. *Rounds and Rounds*. Hargail Music Press, Harold Newman, publisher, 1959. One hundred popular rounds.

Recorder Methods

Burakoff, Gerald and Sonya. *Recorder Time: Method for Group or Individual Instruction*. Sweet Pipes, 23 Scholar Lane, Levittown, NY 11756. Soprano.

King, Carol. *Recorder Routes*. Memphis Musicraft. Soprano.

Kulbach, Johanna and Arthur Nitka. *The Recorder Guild*. Oak Publications. Soprano/alto.

McRae, Shirley W. *Tutoring Tooters*. Memphis Musicraft, 1990. Soprano.

Orr, Hugh. *Basic Recorder Technique*. Berandol. Soprano or alto.

Recorder Ensemble

Benoy, A. W. *Elizabethan and Other Tunes for Recorder Ensemble*. Oxford University Press. SSA/SAT.

Burakoff, Sonya. *Duet Times, Vols. 1 and 2*. Sweet Pipes. SS.

Burakoff, Gerald and Sonya. *Twelve Traditional Christmas Carols*. SAT.

Burakoff, Gerald, and Willie Strickland. *Renaissance Time*. Sweet Pipes. SS, SA, SSA.

———. *The Christmas Album*. Sweet Pipes. SS, SA, SSA.

Katz, Erich, ed. *Old Christmas Songs and Carols*. Hargail Press, SSA, SAT.

Simpson, Kenneth. *Descants in Consort*. Schott edition 10752. SSS.

Whitney, Maurice. *Folk Songs of Europe*. Consort Music. SSA, SST.

Videocassettes

Body, Mind, Spirit, Voice. Concordia. Helen Kemp. 30 min.

The Children's Choir Videotape. American Choral Directors Association on Location, Vol. 1. ACDA, Box 6310, Lawton, OK 73506.

Sing and Rejoice. Concordia. Helen Kemp in rehearsal. 90 min.

Orff Church Collections

Carley, Isabel, ed. *Carols and Anthems, Books I and II*. Mainz: Schott, 1972. Keetman and Orff arrangements; Latin and English texts.

Frazee, Jane. *Ten Folk Carols for Christmas from the United States*. London: Schott, 1977. Orff settings of Appalachian and other American carols.

———. *Singing in the Season*. MMB, 1983. Christmas and Hanukkah songs arranged for voices and Orff instruments.

Goetze, Mary. *Sing We Noel*. St. Louis: MMB, 1984. Six carols, some with Orff instruments, arranged for voices (one–three parts).

McRae, Shirley W. *Celebrate*. Minneapolis: Augsburg, 1984. A collection of church materials arranged for voices and Orff instruments, together with explanation of the pedagogy.

———. *Let Us Praise God*. Minneapolis: Augsburg Fortress, 1989. Hymns and other liturgical material arranged for voices and Orff instruments.

Murray, Margaret. *Four Christmas Carols*. London: Schott. Simple arrangements in Orff style.

———. *Nine Carols*. London: Schott. More advanced material.

Page, Sue Ellen. *Four Psalm Settings*. Schott, 1971. Unison and two-part songs with Orff instruments.

Warner, Brigette, ed. *Jubilate Deo*. Allison Park, PA: Musik Innovation, 1976. Twelve Christmas songs and carols for children's voices, Orff instruments and recorders.

Wuytack, Jos. *Missa Elementaria*. Schott, 1972. Unison to five-part, with optional keyboard. French text. Children, congregation, Orff instruments.

———. *The Ark of Noah*. Memphis: Cockadoodle Tunes, 1982. Short cantata for choir, soloist, recorders, Orff instruments, and movement.

Additional Resources

Recordings of Children's Choirs

Eight Hymns for Our Heritage of Hymns. Bach Choir of the Nassau Presbyterian Church, Princeton, NJ, Sue Ellen Page, Director. Available through the Choristers Guild.

Glen Ellyn Children's Chorus, Doreen Rao, Director. A variety of tapes available from 501 Hill Avenue, Room 202, Glen Ellyn, IL 60137.

Great Hymns for Children. Westwood Choristers, Ron Nelson, Director. Available through Augsburg Publishing House.

Hymn Festival. St. Olaf College Choir and Westwood Choristers. Augsburg.

Sing for Joy. The Winnipeg Mennonite Children's Choir, Helen Litz, Director. Choristers Guild.

Singing the Seasons of the Lord. The Winnipeg Mennonite Children's Choir, Helen Litz, Director. Choristers Guild.

Spirit of Christmas. Toronto Children's Chorus, Jean Ashworth Bartle, Director. 60 St. Clair Avenue, West, Suite 5A, Toronto, Canada M4V 1M7. Other tapes and records available.

With Joyful Hearts. Westwood Choristers, Ron Nelson, Director. Available through Augsburg Publishing House.

Visuals

AMSI Catalog (Art Masters Studios, Inc.), 2614 Nicollet, Minneapolis, MN 55408. Postcards.

Choristers Guild Catalog. Bumper stickers, posters, certificates, bulletin board items, brochures, postcards, bulletin inserts, jewelry, awards.

Mask-charade. 871 Alice St., #12, Monterey, CA 93940. Hundreds of charming felt masks, complete or in kits.

Instruments

Augsburg Fortress Publishing House (Sonor Orff Instruments), 426 South Fifth Street, Box 1209, Minneapolis, MN 55440.

Malmark, Inc., Bell Crest Park, Box 1200, Plumsteadville, PA 18949 (handbells).

MMB Music, Inc. (Studio 49 Orff instruments), 10370 Page Industrial Blvd., St. Louis, MO 63132.

Petit Fritsen Bell Foundry, Bellfounderstreet, Aarle-Rixel, Holland. (US agent: G.I.A., 7404 South Mason Avenue, Chicago, IL 60638 (handbells).

Rhythm Band, Inc. (New Era Orff instruments), 1212 E. Lancaster, P.O. Box 126, Fort Worth, TX 76101.

Schulmerich Carillons, Inc., 177 Carillon Hill, Sellersville, PA 18960 (handbells).

Suzuki Musical Instruments (Suzuki Orff instruments), Suzuki Corporation, P.O. Box 26130, San Diego, CA 92126.

Whitechapel Bell Foundry, 32 & 34 Whitechapel Rd., London E1 1DX, England (handbells).

Stories and Books for Children

De Paola, Tomie. *The Legend of Old Befana.* New York: Harcourt, Brace, Jovanovich, 1980. An Italian Christmas folk tale that lends itself to musical and dramatic development.

————. *The Clown of God.* New York: Harcourt, Brace, Jovanovich, 1978. The ancient legend of the little juggler who offers his own special gift to the Christ Child.

Kuskin, Karla. *The Philharmonic Gets Dressed.* San Francisco: Harper and Row, 1982. The 105 members of the Philharmonic Orchestra prepare for a performance.

L'Engle, Madeleine. *Ladder of Angels.* San Francisco: Harper and Row, 1979. Stories from the Bible illustrated by children of the world.

Mundy, Simon. *The Usborne Story of Music.* London: Usborne Publishers, 1980. Colorful, illustrated brief story of music from ancient times to contemporary.

Stains, Bill. *All God's Critters Got a Place in the Choir.* New York: Dutton, 1978. Beautifully illustrated version of an amusing song.

Voight, Erna, ill. *Peter and the Wolf.* Boston: David R. Godine, n.d. Prokofiev's musical tale brought to life by enchanting illustrations.

Guide to Abbreviations in Orff Arrangements

Pitched

SG = soprano glockenspiel
AG = alto glockenspiel

SM = soprano metallophone
AM = alto metallophone
BM = bass metallophone

SX = soprano xylophone
AX = alto xylophone
BX = bass xylophone
CBB = contrabass tone bar

Unpitched—Membrane

○ = hand drum

⊔ = conga drum

○ = bass drum

○•○ = bongo drum

⋈ = snare drum

⊔ = timpani

V = voices
SR = soprano recorder
AR = alto recorder

S = snap
C = clap
P = patschen
S = stamp

Unpitched—Metal

△ = triangle

◯◯ = finger cymbals

= sleigh bells

⊥ = suspended cymbal

= agogo bells

= gong

= flexatone

▯▯▯▯ = chime bar

= cow bell

= tambourine

Unpitched—Wood

✕ = claves

▭┤▭ = tic toc block

= maracas

= rattle

= piccolo blocks

= whip

= castanets

= cabasa

▯◻▭▯ = temple blocks

▭ = sand blocks

= guiro

= ratchet

= log drum, slit drum

= vibra slap

▭ = wood block

The Church Musician and the Copyright Law

Reprinted by permission
Church Music Publishers Association
P.O. Box 158992
Nashville, TN 37215

This guide does not presume to be a comprehensive summary of the Copyright Act of 1976. It does not attempt to deal with all the issues covered by the legislation, nor does it provide answers to many of the legal questions.

It is intended to be a guide to understanding the nature of copyright by the users of church music to improve their ministries, to maintain a proper standard of ethics, and to help protect themselves and their churches from incurring liability or subjecting themselves to the possibility of being embarrassed or even sued. The questions addressed are the ones which are most frequently asked by church musicians.

A complete copy of the Copyright Law of 1976 and further information regarding the Copyright Law may be obtained by writing: The Copyright Office, Library of Congress, Washington, D.C. 20559.

1. What does "copyright" mean?

Our nation's founding fathers determined that it was in the public interest that the creative works of a person's mind and spirit should belong, for a limited time, to the creator. The protection of these works is called "copyright." The United States Copyright Law grants to any copyright owner the exclusive rights to original material for a term which is *equal to the length of the life of the author/creator plus fifty years.* (For many songs written prior to 1978, the term is 75 years.) The copyright owner is the only one who has the privilege of reproducing the work. If any other party wants to reproduce the material in some manner, permission must be obtained from the copyright owner.

Visible notice of copyright should appear on all copies of copyrighted music, whether on the owner's original works or on permitted copies, the notice should be visible and contain the word "copyright" or the symbol © (for printed material) or p (for sound recordings), the year of first publication and the name of the copyright owner.

2. What are the rights of copyright owners?

A. To reproduce the copyright work in printed copies or on records, tapes, video cassettes, or *any duplicating process* now known or which later comes into being.

B. To make arrangements and adaptations of that copyrighted work.

C. To distribute and/ or sell printed or recorded copies of the work or to license others to do so.

D. To perform the copyrighted work.

E. To display the copyrighted work.

3. Who owns the legal right to make copies?

The original creators (authors and composers) and/or publishers, assigned agents, etc.

4. Do other countries have copyright laws?

Yes. Most of the world now seems to recognize the need to give incentive and protection to creative persons. Copyrighted material owned by U.S. citizens is protected in many other countries by these countries' copyright laws and treaties with the United States.

5. What if I'm faced with a special situation?

If you want to include copyrighted lyrics in a song sheet . . . arrange a copyrighted song for four baritones and kazoo . . . or make any special use of copyrighted music which the publisher cannot supply in regular published form, the magic word is . . . ASK. You may or may not receive permission, but when you use someone else's property you must have the property owner's consent.

6. What if there's not time to write?

Think of copyrighted music as a piece of property, and you'll be on the right track. *Plan ahead.* Some publishers routinely grant permissions over the phone.

7. What about photocopies or tapes that are now in our church?

Immediately destroy any unauthorized photocopies, tapes, etc., and replace them with legal editions. Possession of any illegal copies puts you in the position of harboring stolen goods.

8. Is it permissible to:

- Make a photocopy of a copyrighted work for my accompanist in order to sing a solo?
- Print words only of a copyrighted work on a one-time basis for uses such as church bulletins or song-sheets?
- Print songbooks or song sheets containing copyrighted works and use them in churches, Bible studies, or home prayer groups as long as they are not sold?
- Make a transparency or slide of a copyrighted work for use by a projector?
- Make copies of copyrighted music first and then ask permission?

No. Permission must be secured prior to any such uses and/or duplications.

9. What if I can't find the owner of a copyrighted song, can I go ahead and use it without permission?

No. Check the copyright notice on the work, and/or check with the publisher of the collection in which the work appears. Once you know the name of the copyright owner, write or call the Church Music Publishers Association given above for assistance in locating an address or phone number. For a cost reimbursement of $2, CMPA will supply a current listing of major sacred music copyright holders/publishers. Please send cash. CMPA cannot invoice.

10. But what about items that are out of print?

Most publishers are agreeable, under special circumstances, to allow reprinting of out-of-print items; but again, permission must be secured from the copyright owner prior to any duplication.

11. What is *public domain*?

If a song is in the public domain (P.D.), the copyright protection for the song has expired and the song is dedicated to the public for use as it sees fit with no permission being required from anyone. The absence of a copyright notice (see question 1) is one indication that a song may be P.D.

12. What is *fair use*?

Fair use is not generally available to churches. Fair use is a doctrine developed by the courts which permits portions of copyrighted works to be legally reproduced for purposes of criticism, comment, news reporting, classroom teaching, scholarship, and research. In no instance does this apply to a performance. The various interest groups involved have agreed upon guidelines which constitute the minimum and not the maximum standards of educational fair use.

13. Is it permissible to perform copyrighted religious works in church?

Yes. You may perform copyrighted religious works from legal editions in the course of services at places of worship or at religious assemblies. Legal editions do not result from unauthorized duplication of religious works: i.e., to purchase one copy of religious sheet music, then make 30 copies for the choir without permission and then perform it in a worship service is not legal or ethical.

14. Can I make an original recording of a copyrighted song?

Yes, but you must secure a recording license from the copyright owner, and pay, effective January 1, 1988, a royalty of $5^{1}/_{4}$ cents per song, per record, or tape manufactured. (This rate increases every two years.) *This includes copies of recordings or tapes of church services, concerts, musicals, or any programs that include copyrighted music.*

15. Can I make a record or tape using a prerecorded instrumental accompaniment track?

Yes, provided you have proper permission; and two different permissions are necessary in this situation. The first is from the copyright owner of the selection to be recorded (see Question 13), and the second is from the producer/manufacturer of the accompaniment track. Fees are usually required for each permission.

16. Is it permissible to make duplicates of the tape that accompanies a musical or printed work for "learning" or "rehearsal" purposes?

No, *it is illegal*. As good an idea as this is, and as helpful as it would be to teach the music to members of the choir, it is against the law without permission. Write or call the publisher of the music. They will usually work with you concerning your request.

17. If I buy a record, is it permissible to make a copy for a friend?

Duplications of copyrighted materials is against the law when the purpose avoids a legal purchase.

18. What are the penalties for making unauthorized copies of copyrighted music?

Embarrassment is the first. Additionally, the law provides for the owner of a copyright to recover damages for unauthorized use of copyrighted music. These damages include the profits of the infringer and statutory damages ranging from not less than $250 to not more than $50,000 per infringement. In addition, prison terms are provided for willful (i.e., you knew what you were doing was wrong!) and commercial infringement. Remember, churches, schools and not-for-profit organizations can be infringers too!

19. What about photocopiers who don't get caught?

Frankly, we cannot imagine what kind of school, church or professional musician would derive satisfaction from doing something illegal. They force the price of legal editions higher. They risk embarrassment from professional colleagues who understand the law. They risk fines and jail sentences if taken to court.

Plainly stated, *the making of unauthorized copies of all copyrighted material is strictly illegal.* However, all music publishers desire to have their songs used in as many ways as possible; so in some cases, permission can be obtained. You must contact the copyright owner prior to use or duplication.

On October 19, 1976, President Gerald R. Ford signed into law Public Law 94-553 setting forth the law of the land in regard to copyrights. This new law became effective January 2, 1978.

If you have further questions, contact Church Music Publishers Association, P.O. Box 158992, Nashville, TN 37215, or call (615) 791-0273. This information is furnished through the courtesy of the Church Music Publishers Association.

INDEX